Lord, please help me to change

JUDITH COUCHMAN

WORD PUBLISHING
Dallas·London·Vancouver·Melbourne

LORD, PLEASE HELP ME TO CHANGE

Unless otherwise noted, Scripture quotations are from *The Holy Bible, New Century Version*. Copyright © 1987, 1988, 1991 by Word Publishing.

Other Scripture quotations are from the following sources:

The New American Standard Bible (NASB) © 1960, 1962, 1963, 1968, 1971, 1972, 1973, 1975, 1977 by the Lockman Foundation. Used by permission.

The Amplified Bible (*Amplified*), Copyright © 1965 by Zondervan Publishing House.

Library of Congress Cataloging-in-Publication Data:

Couchman, Judith, 1953–
    Lord, please help me to change / Judith Couchman.
      p. cm.
    Includes selected Bible passages.
    ISBN 0-8499-5011-2
     1. Women—Prayer-books and devotions—English.
  2. Change—Religious aspects—Christianity—Prayer-books and devotionals—English. I. Bible English. New Century. Selections. 1992. II. Title.
    BV4527.C684 1992
    248.8'43—dc20   92–33154
                                     CIP

Printed in the United States of America

3 4 5 9 LB 9 8 7 6 5 4 3 2

For Karen and Jim,
who lovingly help people to change

ALSO BY JUDITH COUCHMAN

Getting a Grip on Guilt
If I'm So Good, Why Don't I Act That Way?
Lord, Have You Forgotten Me?
Why Is Her Life Better Than Mine?

Contents

Acknowledgments

To create the *Heartfelt* series and to write this book it required the talents of many people.

At Word Publishing, I'm grateful to the creative team of Carol Bartley, senior editor, who sincerely cares about writers as people, and Dan Rich, vice president, who keeps opening doors for me professionally. Kudos to them for taking a chance on an unknown author. And to my friend Deena Davis who quickly and expertly copyedited the manuscript.

I'm also grateful to Lauren Libby and Kent Wilson from The Navigators/NavPress who opened doors for me to escape from work and write this book. Without their sensitivity, I'd have never completed it.

I owe a deep thanks to my prayer support group, another team that's crucial to the publishing process: Charette Barta, Opal Couchman, Madalene Harris, Karen Hilt, Shirley Honeywell, Mae Lammers and Nancy Lemons. They prayed me through a short deadline and my first case of writer's block.

I'm also indebted to my niece Melissa Honeywell who researched vague ideas into realistic anecdotes. Someday, she'll write her own books, but in the meantime, I'm delighted with her help.

And thanks to friends near and far who encouraged me to write, despite my stressed personality, unreturned phone calls, and canceled social engagements. A friend to a writer is a friend, indeed.

Introduction

IT'S NEVER TOO LATE

Getting past the fear of trying and failing

For years, I've been an addict without knowing it. What has looked obvious to others has stayed invisible to me. Partly because I haven't known any better. Partly because I've practiced denial. Partly because I've feared that the agony of facing myself would grow too unbearable.

I've been addicted to bolstering my low self-esteem. That may not sound like much, but it's snared me in a subtle but complex web of overdoing it. In the last two decades at one time or another—or all at once—I've overspent, overeaten, overcontrolled, overachieved, and overreacted my way through life. And I've felt pain and remorse because of these actions.

To cope, I chalked up these "over" activities to a creative spirit, until several years ago when my mother stunned me with reality. As lovingly as possible she said, "Judy, you're just dumping things into a big, bottomless hole inside of you." The translation: "You'll never be satisfied until you heal what's hurting internally."

Still, I didn't embark on a pilgrimage toward change right away. It's taken time, trouble, and disappointment to admit my runaway pain and problems and to say, "I need to change."

With that statement I confessed it to myself. With this book I'm admitting it so you can find kinship. In between, I've sometimes successfully and sometimes failingly worked at changing.

*I*f you've felt the pain of discovering a need for personal change, then journey through this book with me. Whether you want to change something "big" or "small," it doesn't matter. These thirty readings address topics common to everyone in the change process, whether it's problems with food or anger or alcohol or time management.

The six parts of this book will help you consider how to:
- step out of denial and into the truth.
- become more realistic about yourself.
- handle the pain and emotions of change.
- survive the ups and downs of transition.
- fight personal battles so you can persevere.
- hold on to the progress you make.

Yet these readings don't deliver step-by-step directions for changing yourself. Nor can they substitute for the inner work you may need to pursue with a counselor. Instead, they're meant to encourage you along the way; to introduce you to the pertinent issues; to help you delve into God's Word as you work at change. They're offered with the advice to "Think about this" rather than the declaration of "Here's the answer!"

As you read the daily selections, it will also help to remember these characteristics of change:

• **Change usually emerges from a process.** Although God performs miracles of immediate change, you'll probably transform through long-term evolution rather than a single event. Even with the miraculous, it's paramount to spiritually and physically guard against losing the instant ground you gain.

• **Change happens in small, day-to-day increments.** It's tempting to look at the big picture—the major obstacles—and try to overcome them with a gigantic leap. That approach doesn't work. Instead, effective change happens with daily choices that don't appear to matter but add up over the months.

• **Change occurs through various creative and unexpected methods.** There's no surefire or one-way means to transformation. The Bible, therapy, support groups, healing prayers, personal discipline, one-to-one accountability, and God's supernatural power all can contribute. God is creative, so stay open to the surprises and internal awakenings He may bestow on you.

Ultimately, the change process works best when it's tailored to who you are rather than what others think you should do.

• **Change never translates into perfection.** As a sinner in a fallen world, with God's help you can manage improvement but not perfection. And since He employs the weak and broken in His service, there may be "thorns in the flesh" (2 Corinthians 12:7) that God chooses never to heal. At this point, you can decide to change your attitude—and that's a miracle in itself!

• **Change requires a lifetime commitment.** Some personal problems resolve quickly; others take years to conquer. One thing remains certain: There's always something that needs to change. Consequently, life balances between accepting your imperfections and choosing to change. Both require a commitment to personal discovery and growth. Both need God's relentless love and guidance.

All told, deep and lasting change cannot occur without the Holy Spirit's touch. So before you begin the change process, ask Him to dissolve your fear of trying and failing; to strengthen and shield you from giving up; to deeply affect what's hurting inside you.

Getting started isn't as difficult as you might think. It begins with a simple request: "Lord, please help me to change."

—*Judith Couchman*

Note: In some readings, the author altered names and circumstances or created composites to protect identities.

Part One

STARTLING INTO THE TRUTH

Stepping out of denial and into the agony

enial allows us to avoid coming to terms with what is really going on inside us and in front of our eyes. I tell my trainees and the people in my workshops to "see what you see and know what you know." When we refuse, we participate in a dishonest system and help to perpetuate it. Many women fear the alternative, however. They think that if they see what they see and know what they know, they will no longer be able to relate to the [people] in their lives. We cannot be alive in a system based upon denial. It leaves us no real avenue to deal with our reality. [1]

Anne Wilson Schaef,
When Society Becomes an Addict

*B*elieve me, when I studied to become a teacher, nobody told me about parent-teacher conferences. If college professors would have explained how nerve-racking these encounters can be, I might have changed my major.

Instead, I became a high-school teacher.

Every quarter I chewed my fingernails past recognition while waiting for the first parents to arrive for an appointment. *Would they be pleasant? Would they be realistic about their child? Would they believe me if I told them bad news about their student?* (We teachers worry about these conferences, too.)

Despite my fretting, most parents proved a delight. Even when I delivered a less than glowing report about their teenager's performance, many parents amicably discussed how we could work together to help him improve.

Only a few parents couldn't believe their child performed less than perfectly in school. And these parents produced my hacked-down fingernails.

I still remember an encounter with Mrs. Smith.

That quarter, her daughter earned a string of "D" and "F" grades on tests and homework for my journalism class. Becca sat glumly through each session, contributing nothing. She mumbled or didn't speak when I talked to her.

So I thought Becca was lucky to find a "D" (a barely passing grade) on her report card.

Mrs. Smith didn't think so.

The moment she sat down, Becca's mom attacked me and my "terrible teaching."

"Becca couldn't possibly deserve a grade like this," she said, and continued her complaint.

As a young and inexperienced teacher, I felt tempted to believe her. But then I noticed Becca's report card sitting on the table between us. She had received "D" and "F" grades in all of her classes.

Mrs. Smith couldn't face the truth.

*W*hy is it so hard to face the truth?

Probably because the truth, like a mirror, reflects reality and what's less-than-beautiful about ourselves.

It's like Saturday morning when I clean house. Since I live alone, I don't worry about what I look like. With no make-up and hair stuck out to there, I dust and scrub in my nightshirt. (Who wants to take a shower first thing in the morning, only to need another dousing when you're through cleaning at noon?)

My system works fine until somebody startles me with the doorbell. Suddenly, I realize I'm a smelly fright.

Do I answer the ring?

Never.

I bolt to a room where, from the front door's perspective, nobody can find me.

That's often what happens when we're confronted by a need to change. Unable to handle what's unsightly about ourselves, we run for cover, hoping no one saw us.

Unfortunately, it's usually too late. Often by the time we "see what we see and know what we know"[2] about ourselves, people around us already recognize our need for change. (Why are we always the last to know?)

Even if we do manage to hide, sooner or later our problems ooze out. And even with the best of cover-ups, there's always somebody who knows everything.

It's God.

And pleasing Him is reason enough to change.

PERSONAL CHECKPOINT

Have you been startled into the truth about yourself? In Part One, consider the debilitating effects of denial and how to begin the journey toward change.

1. What would you like to change about yourself?

2. How did it feel to discover this need for change?

3. What was your first response to this need for change? Why did you respond this way?

Day 1

EVERYDAY LIES

**We begin to change by forsaking denial
and telling the truth about ourselves.**

Aimee remembers when the lies began. But it took desperate circumstances to recognize the half-truths she told about her out-of-control spending.

"My parents didn't teach me about money. But that didn't motivate me, as an adult, to read or take lessons on how to manage it," she says. "I just thought that somehow, magically, I'd do okay with it."

For a while, it did feel magical. When Aimee graduated from college, finance companies and department stores sent her instant-credit applications. Other businesses didn't even ask her to apply: They just mailed plastic cards to her.

"It felt like heaven," she remembers. "Without cash, I could buy the things I needed for my apartment. At first I felt cautious, but then I told myself it was all right to spend up to every card's limit. I assured myself that if they sent me the cards, I could afford them."

But Aimee had lied to herself. When the bills arrived, a twenty-year cycle of overspending and lying and struggling began.

"At first I didn't suffer much. I could pay the credit-card bills—or at least the monthly minimums—and then scrimp on other things. But then I started missing payments and making up for them the next month," she explains.

"When I paid bills, I vowed to change. But when I got in the stores, I'd tell myself it was okay to buy more things. Or that this one more thing wouldn't matter; I could control myself after that."

She pauses and then admits, "Those were lies to make me feel better. And I told them to myself for years."

Aimee survived the cycle for a while. But gradually and painfully, those generous companies wrote collection letters and revoked her credit cards because of late payments. Yet not even that prompted her to change.

"Who knows what I was thinking then?" she asks. "I probably didn't change because my secret felt safe—just between me and the faceless credit-card people. And I told myself, for the umpteenth time, that I'd reform."

Instead, Aimee overspent her checkbook. Eventually, she bounced so many checks that the bank closed her account. More than once, the telephone and utility companies disconnected their services for nonpayment. Periodically, she paid the rent late, and after paying bills, she lived on a few dollars for two weeks.

"I remember eating crackers for dinner and not thinking much of it. Instead of jolting me into reality, the self-lies numbed me to it," Aimee says. "I limped along for a long time before I wanted to change."

Aimee can't pinpoint when reality began to seep in. But eventually, she got so sick of her lifestyle she had to change.

"I saw other people with peace of mind, good credit ratings, and the ability to have homes and savings accounts," she says. "Maybe that's when I faced the lying to myself—and the ruin it had brought me to. I had squandered myself on lots of small things and missed the big things I'd really wanted. That's when I admitted my sin to God and told Him I was ready to change."

She adds: "I'm in the process of changing now, and every day I fight the old lies I've told myself, and I replace them with the truth. For example, when I say, 'Buying this one thing won't matter,' I remind myself that it does matter if I can't really afford it."

*L*ike many of us, Aimee fell into a pit before recognizing her need to change. Landing with nothing to soften the blow, she faced the enormity of her self-lies. On the surface, they had looked harmless, inconsequential. But peering at them face-to-face below, she couldn't deny their repugnance.

"Denial runs deep. We tell ourselves lies," wrote Melody Beattie, who practiced denial for years. "When some awareness, some reality, threatens to hurt us, we trick ourselves into believing 'it ain't so.'. . . People deny just about anything that can be denied—but what we usually deny is what we have lost, are losing, or suspect we're losing—something important to us." [3]

Aimee denied the truth for fear she'd lose the personal image she longed to project. She wanted to be a woman who "had it all," including the admiration of others and respect for herself. Ironically, those self-lies garnered the opposite of her dreams.

As the father of lies, that's exactly what Satan wants: to make the truth sound as lies—and lies to ring as the truth. He'll mire us in his pit as long as we allow it, but there's really no need to wallow there. We can reach up, grasp the Shepherd's hand, and together begin the journey toward change.

He only requires that we tell the truth.

PERSONAL CHECKPOINT

1. What lies do you tell yourself? Why?

2. If you face the truth, what are you afraid of losing?

GOD'S VIEWPOINT

John writes about the nature of truth:

Here is the message we have heard from Christ and now announce to you: God is light, and in him there is no darkness at all. So if we say we have fellowship with God, but we continue living in darkness, we are liars and do not follow the truth. But if we live in the light, as God is in the light, we can share fellowship with each other. Then the blood of Jesus, God's Son, cleanses us from every sin.

If we say we have no sin, we are fooling ourselves, and the truth is not in us. But if we confess our sins, he will forgive our sins, because we can trust God to do what is right. He will cleanse us from all the wrongs we have done. If we say we have not sinned, we make God a liar, and we do not accept God's teaching.

My dear children, I write this letter to you so you will not sin. But if anyone does sin, we have a helper in the presence of the Father—Jesus Christ, the One who does what is right. He is the way our sins are taken away, and not only our sins but the sins of all people.

We can be sure that we know God if we obey his commands. Anyone who says, "I know God," but does not obey God's commands is a liar, and the truth is not in that person. But if someone obeys God's teaching, then in that person God's love has truly reached its goal. This is how we can be sure we are living in God: Whoever says that he lives in God must live as Jesus lived.

—1 John 1:5—2:6

YOUR RESPONSE

1. How can you infuse God's truth into your life?

2. How can this truth help you to change?

Day 2

DON'T SHOOT THE MESSENGER

Sometimes God uses other people to confirm our need to change.

ou know, your competitive attitude has caused problems with your friends," she ventured while sitting at my dining room table, watching me iron clothes in the kitchen.

"What?" I shot back. "Who told you that? You don't even live in this town! You're never around me long enough to know what I'm like." I wanted to throw the iron at her.

Hurt and furious, I closed down the conversation as quickly as possible. She planned to stay the weekend and I didn't want to spend it fighting. So I composed myself and played the gracious hostess, even though I felt horrible.

Back then, confrontation didn't seem like the "nice" thing to do, especially to a friend. So when this woman confronted me, I interpreted it as disloyalty and rejection. However, in the next year her comment prompted me to evaluate my attitudes and uncover a need for change. The discovery felt painful, but it's beginning to reap precious rewards in relationships and personal satisfaction.

Slowly, I'm learning that if you don't shoot the messenger, she might prove valuable.

*S*omewhere in folklore or history, a messenger delivered bad news and got slaughtered for it. But who killed the messenger and exactly why? Nobody seems to know.

Somebody suggested the biblical story of David killing the man who announced Saul's death, but the real reason centered on the messenger's boasting of personally killing Saul (2 Samuel 1:1-15). Others have nominated the Greeks, the Persians, Pharaoh, and Nebuchadnezzar as messenger killers. In any event, the saying, "Don't shoot the messenger," applies when we receive unfortunate news and rail at somebody who's only a courier.

"I well believe it, to unwilling ears; None love the messenger who brings bad news," wrote Sophocles in his play *Antigone*.[4] Middle management will confirm how difficult the role of a go-between can be. Or police officers who deliver death announcements to unsuspecting families. And God help the IRS clerk.

Nobody wants to bear bad tidings. But to use another cliché, somebody's got to do it. In fact, God has employed middle men and women for centuries. Noah's ark warned of a coming flood. Moses blasted the Israelites for their golden calf. Esther saved a nation by approaching the king. Jeremiah begged God's people to repent. Jesus walked the earth for three years, preaching about eternal judgment.

In these and other biblical incidents, a messenger risked life itself to deliver dire news—and the receivers' response determined their fate and relationship with God.

Hopefully, people who deliver messages to us don't risk as much as those in the Old and New Testaments. But the risk in our response looms just as great. We can receive the truth about ourselves with gratefulness—or suffer the consequences of sin and woundedness.

When we greet these messengers as allies, we also welcome the Friend who "sticks closer than a brother" (Proverbs 18:24), the one who holds the power to truly change us.

❦

PERSONAL CHECKPOINT

1. Has someone pinpointed your need to change?

2. Is there truth in this person's words?

GOD'S VIEWPOINT

Words to the wise about messengers:

The right word spoken at the right time
is as beautiful as gold apples in a silver bowl.

A wise warning to someone who will listen
is as valuable as gold earrings or fine gold jewelry.

Trustworthy messengers refresh those who send them,
like the coolness of snow in the summertime.

People who brag about gifts they never give
are like clouds and wind that give no rain.

With patience you can convince a ruler,
and a gentle word can get through to the hard-
headed.

Don't brag about tomorrow;
you don't know what may happen then.

Don't praise yourself. Let someone else do it.
Let the praise come from a stranger and not from
your own mouth.

Stone is heavy, and sand is weighty,
but a complaining fool is worse than either.

Anger is cruel and destroys like a flood,
but no one can put up with jealousy!

It is better to correct someone openly
than to have love and not show it.

The slap of a friend can be trusted to help you,
but the kisses of an enemy are nothing but lies.

When you are full, not even honey tastes good,
but when you are hungry, even something bitter
tastes sweet.

A person who leaves his home
  is like a bird that leaves its nest.

The sweet smell of perfume and oils is pleasant,
  and so is good advice from a friend.

Don't forget your friend or your parent's friend.
  Don't always go to your family for help when trouble
  comes.
  A neighbor close by is better than a family far away.

Be wise, my child, and make me happy.
  Then I can respond to any insult.

The wise see danger ahead and avoid it,
  but fools keep going and get into trouble.

Take the coat of someone who promises to pay a
  stranger's loan,
  and keep it until he pays what the stranger owes.

If you loudly greet your neighbor early in the morning,
  he will think of it as a curse.

A quarreling wife is as bothersome
  as a continual dripping on a rainy day.
Stopping her is like stopping the wind
  or trying to grab oil in your hand.

As iron sharpens iron,
  so people can improve each other.
                              —*Proverbs 25:11-15; 27:1-17*

YOUR RESPONSE

1. How can you know whom to trust as a messenger of change?

2. How can you welcome a messenger of change as a friend?

WHEN YOU
PREFER NOT TO

Refusing to change often damages ourselves and those around us.

I am a man who, from his youth upwards, has been filled with a profound conviction that the easiest way of life is the best," began the narrator in Herman Melville's short story, "Bartleby the Scrivener." The narrator described himself as an "unambitious lawyer" and an "eminently *safe* man" who never argued a court case and catered to the wills and other legal needs of the wealthy. [5]

At the turn of the century, this lawyer employed scriveners, men who copied legal documents by hand. A common practice involved one man reading from the original document while others checked their copied versions for accuracy.

That was the fun part. Most of the time, scriveners kept their heads bent over detailed manuscripts, copying. Thus, the lawyer and his two copyists carried on business in a monotonous and predictable manner.

They weren't prepared for Bartleby.

Business grew, and the lawyer hired Bartleby to assist with copying. At first, Bartleby spent long hours writing, day and night, in a sullen, mechanical manner. The lawyer didn't mind, though, because volumes of work got done. But then the lawyer asked Bartleby to examine a small paper with him.

"I would prefer not to," replied Bartleby.

Stunned, the lawyer continued his busy day. Business demanded his attention; there wasn't time to consider Bartleby's disobedience.

A week later, the lawyer summoned his copyists to double-check four documents from a week of court testimonies. Bartleby appeared from behind his office screen and announced, "I would prefer not to." And no amount of persuasion from the boss changed his preference.

Time and again, when the lawyer requested Bartleby's assistance, the copyist responded with "I would prefer not to." Gradually, Bartleby preferred not to work, not to talk, not to move from his desk, not to leave the office. In fact, by accident the lawyer discovered that Bartleby had turned the office into his living quarters at night and on weekends.

"Nothing so aggravates an earnest person as a passive resistance," the lawyer admitted. Still, he good-heartedly tried to help the maladjusted employee by reasoning with him, expressing compassion, and offering assistance.

Bartleby preferred not to respond to his employer's help. He also preferred not to leave when the lawyer, with no options left, fired him.

In desperation, the lawyer finally moved his practice out of the building, leaving Bartleby to sit alone in an empty room. Later, he discovered that Bartleby had been booted to the building's hallway, where he preferred not to budge, not to eat, not to accept assistance.

However, the police preferred to move Bartleby into prison, where he died from inertia and starvation.

Melville's story speaks to the power of resistance and the perplexing nature of humanity. We resist what's best for us and plunge deeper into trouble.

"I'm too old to change."

"I'll start my diet tomorrow."

"Nobody can tell me what to do!"

"I don't need help from anyone."

"I don't drink as much as she does."

These words emerge from resisters. These people have parted with denial, but they're not going anywhere, either. They realize there's a problem, but they're not tackling it. And they're certainly not planning to change.

Resisters believe that if they maintain the status quo they'll be safe and acceptable, at least to themselves. Granted, they may not like the problem they clutch, but in their minds it's easier to "put a cap on it" than to dismantle and change it. Their motto could be, "No gain, no pain."

Except that's not what really happens.

Personal problems don't just maintain. They usually grow worse if we ignore them. They don't stay just our problems either. They affect and hurt others. Consequently, resisters discover that days or months or years later they're behaving worse than ever before—and people have grown less tolerant of them.

Resisters feel afraid. They fear leaving behind what's familiar, losing a habit's pleasure, or failing to change. So before embarking on change, resisters need time to face their fears.

All of us play the resister at some time or other. But God can strengthen us to resist our fears instead of avoiding the need for change. "Remember that I commanded you to be strong and brave," He said. "Don't be afraid, because the LORD your God will be with you everywhere you go" (Joshua 1:9).

❧

PERSONAL CHECKPOINT

1. Are you resistant to change? If so, why?

2. When trying to change, what scares you the most?

GOD'S VIEWPOINT

King David exalts the Lord's strength and protection:

The ways of God are without fault;
the LORD's words are pure.
He is a shield to those who trust him.

Who is God? Only the LORD.
 Who is the Rock? Only our God.
God is my protection.
 He makes my way free from fault.
He makes me like a deer that does not stumble;
 he helps me stand on the steep mountains.
He trains my hands for battle
 so my arms can bend a bronze bow.
You protect me with your saving shield.
 You have stooped to make me great.
You give me a better way to live,
 so I live as you want me to.
I chased my enemies and destroyed them.
 I did not quit till they were destroyed.
I destroyed and crushed them
 so they couldn't rise up again.
 They fell beneath my feet.
You gave me strength in battle.
 You made my enemies bow before me.

The LORD lives!
 May my Rock be praised!
 Praise God, the Rock, who saves me!
God gives me victory over my enemies
 and brings people under my rule.
He frees me from my enemies.

So I will praise you, LORD, among the nations.
 I will sing praises to your name.
          —2 Samuel 22:31-40, 47-49a, 50

God did not give us a spirit that makes us afraid but a spirit of power and love and self-control.
          —2 Timothy 1:7

YOUR RESPONSE

1. What enemies approach as you move toward change?

2. How can God strengthen you for battle against these foes?

Day 4

NAKED WITH NOWHERE TO RUN

When we uncover our need to change, we can feel emotionally undone.

alk to women who've stayed overnight in a hospital, and they'll describe the humiliations thereof.

First, there's the hospital gown, making us aware of our backsides as never before. Personally, I think those gowns are part of a medical conspiracy to keep patients in bed. Who wants to roam the halls—or even cross the room—in one of those things?

But just when we've grown accustomed to the breeze, the situation gets worse. We regress to wearing a sheet.

At this stage—whether for tests or childbirth or surgery—there's all manner of personal exposure while doctors prod us. And no matter how hard we try to stave them off, they'll eventually pull back the cover and say hello.

I learned this by experience.

In a whirlwind, I checked into the hospital only hours after a dermatologist discovered malignant melanoma growing on my upper right arm. The surgeon scheduled me for his knife the next morning. In the meantime, a parade of doctors and interns visited me to examine the mole that had grown cancerous.

"Wish I'd been this popular in high school," I quipped, trying to stay calm and feeling relieved when they left.

Later that evening, my surgeon's intern assistant strolled into the room. "I'm here to see the mole on your shoulder," he announced. I didn't like his bedside manner, but I pulled out my arm for display. He scrutinized it.

"I understand you also have a mole to be removed from under your breast," he said.

I did. *But there's no way I'll show it to you,* I thought. My surgeon, a fatherly type, hovered around age sixty. The intern looked about my age and far from paternal.

"Yes, I do have a mole there," I replied and crossed my arms over my chest.

He got the message and left.

I congratulated myself for keeping my private parts private. Until the next morning. Rolled into surgery, it suddenly hit me: to remove the second mole, a team of doctors would strip me to the waist.

I've spent my life covering up, and in a few moments these guys will expose me in one swoop, I thought, as the anesthesia kicked in. *Years of modesty destroyed.*

As I drifted toward sleep, the last face I remembered was that of the surgeon's assistant, ready to pull back the sheet and look. Soon I'd be naked with nowhere to run.

*N*aked with nowhere to run. That's how it feels when we first become aware of our need to change. Suddenly, the problem we've denied uncovers itself. We feel exposed and ashamed. We want to escape.

Consequently, we might also feel touchy, weepy, angry, depressed, embarrassed, or otherwise emotionally out of control. Self-discovery can hit with sudden impact. We can reel from the blow.

For example, when a friend of mine discovered that she needed to change herself to alter a debilitating relationship, she wept at unpredictable moments. Another friend facing his bad habits wrestled with bouts of anger. After a house guest confronted me about my competitive spirit, I felt engulfed by shame.

At this point, when we're emotionally raw and unable to help ourselves, it's all right—even necessary—to find shelter.

Finding shelter isn't escaping or ignoring the problem. It's suffering through our ignited emotions in a place where it's safe to express them—with people who will comfort, understand, and when we're steadier, encourage us to begin changing.

Finding shelter also requires a measure of discipline. When emotions spill, we're tempted to talk to anyone who'll listen—friends, coworkers, family members, acquaintances at church, even strangers. In return, we're deluged with advice and opinions that eventually confuse more than nurture us. It takes discipline to choose a few people whom we can trust and stick with them—people who'll love and respect us, no matter what they know about us.

Above all, finding shelter means turning to the God who longs to hide us under the shadow of His wings (Psalm 17:8). When people fail us, when we fail ourselves, He's ever loving, ever accepting, ever listening, ever ready to help us heal and change.

❧

PERSONAL CHECKPOINT

1. Describe the type of person you'd like to find shelter with when you're emotionally vulnerable.

2. Who fits this description? Could you ask this person to help you?

GOD'S VIEWPOINT

Prayer and praise for God's help:

> *God, save me,*
> *because the water has risen to my neck.*
> *I'm sinking down into the mud,*
> *and there is nothing to stand on.*
> *I am in deep water,*
> *and the flood covers me.*
> *I am tired from calling for help;*

my throat is sore.
God, you know what I have done wrong;
I cannot hide my guilt from you.
Lord GOD, All-Powerful,
do not let those who hope in you be ashamed because
of me.
God of Israel, do not let your worshipers be disgraced
because of me.
For you, I carry this shame,
and my face is covered with disgrace.

But I pray to you, LORD, for favor.
God, because of your great love, answer me.
You are truly able to save.
LORD, answer me because your love is so good.
Because of your great kindness, turn to me.

I am sad and hurting.
God, save me and protect me.

I will praise God in a song
and will honor him by giving thanks.
That will please the LORD more than offering him
cattle,
more than sacrificing a bull with horns and hoofs.
Poor people will see this and be glad.
Be encouraged, you who worship God.
The LORD listens to those in need
and does not look down on captives.
—Psalm 69:1-3a, 5-7, 13, 16, 29-33

YOUR RESPONSE

1. During emotionally difficult times, do you cry to God for help? Why, or why not?

2. How can you learn to praise God during these times?

NOBODY SAID IT'D BE EASY

Change is hard work, but the Lord offers us His power for the task.

M ost people who've tackled personal change call it four-letter words. It's H-A-R-D. It's W-O-R-K.

Yes, change requires hard work—a commitment not to give up when it's difficult. But don't take my word for it. Read what other people have said about our part in the change process:

> You are responsible for your actions. You will never receive healing . . . until you *stop blaming everyone else and accept your responsibility.* . . . Do you really want to be healed, or do you just want to talk about your problem? [6]
>
> —David Seamands

> One of the greatest ways God changes me is by bringing Scripture to mind I have hidden deep in my heart. . . . What a reason for *staying in His Word daily—reading, studying, devouring it.* And then what a challenge to *stay so sensitive to the Holy Spirit's speaking* that He can

reach down and recall just exactly what I need at the very minute I need it! [7]

—Evelyn Christenson

The steadfast spirit that enables us to walk the flat country of the heart, whether the skies are gray or clear, doesn't appear overnight. When God rebuilds a gutted life, He builds it a brick at a time. Resilient endurance is the badge of people under construction. . . . the person with a steadfast spirit is *actively willing to remain under pressure of any kind,* as long as God wills, in order to grow stronger.

Blessed is the person who wants growth so badly, that [she] refuses to shrink from the process that produces it. [8]

—David Swartz

Jesus is telling us to feel everything. To be spiritually alive is not to be dead to hurt and pain, but to be free to experience them, trusting God to bring us through them safely.

We need the dark nights, sleepless and agonizing as they are. We need the hurts that keep us tender and the unexplained sorrows that stretch our faith and trust. Living through them will make us different people—and the difference can be good. [9]

—Colleen Townsend Evans

Our very mistakes and our sins, *if we repent of them,* will be used of God to help us in the growth and upbuilding of our character. In the hot fires of penitence we leave the dross and come again as pure gold. But we must remember that it is only Christ who can make our sins yield blessing. [10]

—J. R. Miller

*Y*es, change requires work. But God promises His presence and power to help us persevere. Read what He's said about His role in the process:

God has said, "I will never leave you; I will never forget you." So we can be sure when we say, "I will not be afraid, because the Lord is my helper. People can't do anything to me."

—Hebrews 13:5b-6

My grace is enough for you. When you are weak, my power is made perfect in you.

—2 Corinthians 12:9

God can do all things. I tell you the truth, if your faith is as big as a mustard seed, you can say to this mountain, "Move from here to there," and it will move. All things will be possible for you.

—Matthew 19:26b; 17:20b–c

I will give her peace that will flow to her like a river. I will comfort you as a mother comforts her child.

—Isaiah 66: 12a, 13a

God is greater than any difficulty or any amount of hard work we'll pass through as we begin to change.

PERSONAL CHECKPOINT

1. How do you feel about the work that change requires?

2. For you, what is the most difficult part of the change process?

GOD'S VIEWPOINT

Praise to the God who helps His children:

> *I asked the LORD for help, and he answered me.*
> *He saved me from all that I feared.*
> *Those who go to him for help are happy,*
> *and they are never disgraced.*

*This poor man called, and the L*ORD *heard him*
and saved him from all his troubles.
*The angel of the L*ORD *camps around those who fear*
God,
and he saves them.

*Examine and see how good the L*ORD *is.*
Happy is the person who trusts him.
*You who belong to the L*ORD*, fear him!*
Those who fear him will have everything they need.
Even lions may get weak and hungry,
*but those who look to the L*ORD *will have every good*
thing.

*The L*ORD *sees the good people*
and listens to their prayers.
*But the L*ORD *is against those who do evil;*
he makes the world forget them.
*The L*ORD *hears good people when they cry out to him,*
and he saves them from all their troubles.
*The L*ORD *is close to the brokenhearted,*
and he saves those whose spirits have been crushed.

People who do what is right may have many problems,
*but the L*ORD *will solve them all.*
—Psalm 34:4-10, 15-19

YOUR RESPONSE

1. How can you draw on God's power to change?

2. From today's reading, which Scripture encourages you the most? Memorize it for help during the days ahead.

Part Two

A True View of You

Getting realistic about yourself

F ocusing on ourselves takes a number of forms. We can become self-protective, refusing to take risks. We can develop an elaborate system of self-righteousness, denying that we make mistakes in the first place and blaming others for our difficulties. We can become self-consumed, eaten up with guilt for every real and supposed error. But each of these self-centered approaches has the same results: we do not deal honestly with failure, and we carry the weight of our past actions.

When we focus on God, the scene changes. He's in control of our lives; nothing lies outside the realm of His redemptive grace. Even when we make mistakes, fail in relationships, or deliberately make bad choices, God can redeem us. [11]

Penelope J. Stokes,
So What If You've Failed?

I still cringe when I picture it.

Back when malls were new and a curiosity, it stood in front of the shopping center's shoe store where Mom bought her girls those sensible Hush Puppy shoes.

To walk down the mall, I couldn't get around it. And to shop for shoes, well, that really bothered me.

I'm sure the shoe store owner placed it there to attract customers. But it revolted me.

It was a mirror.

But not just any mirror.

This mirror distorted people's bodies, making them appear grotesquely fat. In my opinion, mirrors like that needed to stay where they belonged, in front of circus tents. Instead, it irreverently created havoc in front of an otherwise sedate store.

Many times I had watched other kids stand in front of that mirror, laughing and making fun of their blown-up bellies and behinds.

I couldn't.

I had struggled with a weight problem since childhood. *So why should I make myself look heavier?* I thought. That mirror represented my worst nightmare about personal appearance. It surfaced my fear of someday actually growing that fat.

It was silly, I know. Even back then I thought my feelings were ridiculous. But it didn't change my hatred of that mirror— and my unhappiness with my body.

Ironically, when I look at photos of myself from those years, I would love to be that slim again. When it concerns body image, I've seldom viewed myself accurately.

*N*ot long ago, I laughed over a cartoon of a man and woman, each looking into a mirror. He's fat and slovenly but imagines a taut, muscular man smiling back at him. She's slim and attractive but sees a chunky, homely woman instead of her true reflection.

I'll demur from commentary about men, but I must admit it's tough for women to assess themselves realistically. And for many of us, it's no laughing matter. The pressure cooker of trying to "have it all" spewed us out, but we're not yet sure where we've landed. In our minds, we're still faintly chanting, "I've got to be perfect."

But none of us are.

Consequently, when we decide to change, we may first need to adjust our vision and get realistic. It's possible to emerge from denial and still set goals built on fantasy. However, with God's help, we can view ourselves through His loving and truth-filled eyes.

God knows we're dust and He still loves us. He knows that we're filthy from sin, but He still welcomes us into His arms. He knows that we'll never be perfect on earth, but He still forgives and changes us.

I smile when I picture it. I relax when I understand it. I change when I grasp it.

You can, too.

PERSONAL CHECKPOINT

In Part Two, learn how realism plays a role in the change process—and how it can affect you.

1. Generally, are you realistic about yourself? Why, or why not?

2. Write out your goal(s) to change. How realistic are they? How realistic is the time frame in which you expect to change?

3. How can you stay realistic as you work toward change?

Day 6

FALSE STARTS AND FUMBLES

In our first attempts to change, it's normal to falter and fail.

Katharine Angell was the right woman in the right place at the right time. On the recommendation of a friend—and despite her youth and inexperience—the recently launched *New Yorker* magazine hired her as an editor.

Katharine's insight and attention to detail authenticated the recommendation.

Not long after, she married *New Yorker* author E. B. White. In their later years and her retirement, the Whites hired a secretary to help with the volumes of work and correspondence resulting from forty years of marriage and publishing.

By this time, Katharine had succumbed to poor health and a dramatic change in personality. She grew difficult and her perfectionistic tendencies ballooned into obsessions. Voluminous and detailed correspondence—a strong suit in Katharine's days as an editor—grew to irritate even her devoted husband.

Katharine needed to change.

Valiantly, she attempted changing during her favorite time of year for letter writing: the Christmas season.

A big mistake.

E. B. and Katharine worked through their Christmas list and cut nearly seventy names. Their secretary, Isabel, took these names, each written on an index card, and tied them together with a rubber band. Isabel kept the cast-off list within reach, though, because she suspected a turn of events.

Isabel was right.

A few days later, Katharine asked for the banished cards. She read the list to E. B. again and explained why each name deserved reinstatement.

According to Isabel, "E. B. bowed to the inevitable and retreated, glowering, to his study." [12]

Another year, Katharine again decided to hack back the sacred Christmas list. Her reason: She and E. B. couldn't afford the expense. Then she mailed letters to the rejected names on the list, explaining that she wouldn't be sending Christmas greetings to them.

*E*ven with the best of intentions, we often fail in our first efforts to change. Old habits don't die without a fight. They grab any opportunity to seize us again.

We're especially vulnerable at these times:

• **When we're starting out.** With any new skill, hardly anyone gets it right the first time. It takes practice, practice, practice. And after a blunder, gathering up ourselves and starting over again.

We need reality checks to remind ourselves that multiple failures precede a much-wanted success. Champions learn to recover their fumbles.

• **When we choose the wrong time.** Obviously, Katharine picked a poor time of year to change. She loved Christmas, so it was particularly difficult for her to cut back on correspondence then. Plus, the holiday season always fills up with pressure, and it's difficult to change when we're already stressed.

When we embark on change, it helps to choose a time when other aspects of life run relatively smoothly. (That's not always possible, but we can still consider a time that's at least slightly better than others.)

• **When we're uncertain about our resolve.** Sometimes we begin the change process halfheartedly. We feel that we should, but we don't really want to. That's a prescription for an immediate downfall. How badly do we want to change? The answer determines how steadfastly we stay on course.

Jesus said, "Anyone who begins to plow a field but keeps looking back is of no use in the kingdom of God" (Luke 9:62). Likewise, we can hardly expect to change when we're not looking ahead, focused on the goal.

Later, Paul told the Corinthians: "The one who plows and the one who works in the grain should hope to get some of the grain for their work" (1 Corinthians 9:10c). The same verse in another version of the Bible says we should "plow in hope" (KJV). In this regard, our hope rests in what's ahead rather than what we've left behind.

When we embark on the road to change, we can remember Lot's wife. Fleeing the wickedness of Sodom and Gomorrah, she looked back and turned into a pillar of salt (Genesis 19:26). How much better to keep looking ahead and eventually to taste the sweetness of success.

PERSONAL CHECKPOINT

1. Reread the three ways that we're vulnerable when embarking on change. Do any of these describe you?

2. What can you do to become less vulnerable in these or other areas?

GOD'S VIEWPOINT

A prayer for perseverance:

> *LORD, hear my prayer;*
> *listen to my cry for mercy.*
> *Answer me*
> *because you are loyal and good.*
> *Don't judge me, your servant,*
> *because no one alive is right before you.*

I remember what happened long ago;
I consider everything you have done.
I think about all you have made.
I lift my hands to you in prayer.
As a dry land needs rain, I thirst for you.

LORD, answer me quickly,
because I am getting weak.
Don't turn away from me,
or I will be like those who are dead.
Tell me in the morning about your love,
because I trust you.
Show me what I should do,
because my prayers go up to you.
LORD, save me from my enemies;
I hide in you.
Teach me to do what you want,
because you are my God.
Let your good Spirit
lead me on level ground.
LORD, let me live
so people will praise you.
In your goodness
save me from my troubles.
In your love defeat my enemies.
Destroy all those who trouble me,
because I am your servant.
                    —Psalm 143: 1-2, 5-12

YOUR RESPONSE

1. What part(s) of this prayer can you identify with today?

2. In regard to looking ahead to change, what would you like to say to God? Tell Him in a prayer.

THIS ONE THING I DO

When we tackle several changes at once, we can wind up changing nothing at all.

y watch pointed to 6:30 A.M., which explained part, but not all, of my grogginess. Visiting my hometown on vacation, I had just driven Mom to work so I could use her car for shopping later.

While waiting for a red light to change, my mind wandered to an article I had left on my desk five hundred miles away. Rewriting it in my head, I half-noticed two vehicles pulling around me and driving off. A man in a pickup truck tossed me a weird look as he sped by. I considered returning the favor, but glanced up at the street light instead.

Green. But in a few moments it turned red.

_Oh no,_ I thought. _I just sat through a green light!_

I slouched in the driver's seat, overcome by the demise of my resolve to relax. Even though I had left my briefcase behind, the manuscript had trailed me to Omaha, captured my thoughts, and driven me to distraction instead of down the street. Now my face felt as red as the light smirking above me.

Ask family and friends, and they'll tell you about my penchant for taking on too many projects and getting stressed out.

One personality test describes my type as always wanting "an extra squeeze out of life." That's fine by me, but I don't know how to stop squeezing before I drain the life out of myself.

I seldom recognize when enough is enough.

So that day in the car, I knew missing a stoplight—or even thinking about an article—wasn't the real problem. The incident simply indicated that, once again, I had taken on too much in too little time.

Considering my bent toward overdoing it, it's easy to imagine how I've attempted personal change in the past: I've tried to alter too many things at once. And that's a surefire way to fail.

To accomplish a task well, we need to focus.

Focus means we concentrate on only one goal.

That's difficult for many of us. We're a generation of daily planner users, management-by-objective employees, and New Year's resolution writers. We make lists and expect to complete them in rapid-fire succession. We think that the more we handle, the more respected and successful we'll be.

We're also a people of burnout and emotional breakdowns. We don't know how to focus.

One of my friends, a career pianist, has helped me to understand focus. It began with an incident in college when we lived together. I spent days studying for a test, taking numerous breaks, letting my mind wander, and nodding off to sleep. The night before the test, Nancy entered our room after 10 P.M., pulled out the textbook, and began reading several chapters for the test— for the first time. True to form, I fell asleep before she finished.

The next morning we both took the test. Nancy received an "A" and I got a low "B."

We're both smart women, but Nancy knows how to focus. Twenty years later, I'm reminded of that when I see her leaning into the piano, hands a blur over the keyboard, filling the room with magnificent sounds.

Me? I'm late getting this manuscript to my editor. I'm a slow learner on the subject of focus.

But in the past few years I've accepted that I can only handle one change at a time. While I work on managing money better, it's not wise for me also to diet. I risk getting too frustrated and giving up on both. (I've done that in the past.)

Actually, God didn't create us to be jugglers. He designed us with one goal in mind: to please Him. Except sin muddled up the plan—and the rat race began.

Midst the clutter, though, God still calls individuals to one task at a time. To Moses: "Go save my people." To the prophets: "Preach the truth." To Mary: "Raise my Son." Even Jesus focused on one goal: to do the will of His Father in heaven. And the apostle Paul said, "This one thing I do" instead of "These fourteen things I do and choke on most of them."

While these biblical examples represent God's call to lifetime tasks, there's a principle that trickles down into the everyday. To achieve what matters—and to really change—we need to focus.

With Paul we can say, "I know that I have not yet reached that goal, but there is one thing I always do. Forgetting the past and straining toward what is ahead, I keep trying to reach the goal" (Philippians 3:13–14a).

❧

Personal Checkpoint

1. How are you doing at focusing on your goal to change?

2. How might you narrow and sharpen your focus?

God's Viewpoint

On developing focus:

I do not mean that I am already as God wants me to be. I have not yet reached that goal, but I continue trying to reach it and to make it mine. Christ wants me to do that, which is the reason he made me his. Brothers and sisters, I know that I have not yet reached that goal, but there is one thing I always do. Forgetting the past and straining toward what is ahead, I keep trying to reach the goal and get the prize for which God called me through Christ to the life above.

All of us who are spiritually mature should think this way, too. And if there are things you do not agree with, God will make them clear to you. But we should continue following the truth we already have.

Brothers and sisters, all of you should try to follow my example and to copy those who live the way we showed you. Many people live like enemies of the cross of Christ. I have often told you about them, and it makes me cry to tell you about them now. In the end, they will be destroyed. They do whatever their bodies want, they are proud of their shameful acts, and they think only about earthly things. But our homeland is in heaven, and we are waiting for our Savior, the Lord Jesus Christ, to come from heaven. By his power to rule all things, he will change our simple bodies and make them like his own glorious body.

Be full of joy in the Lord always. I will say again, be full of joy.
—Philippians 3:12-21, 4:4

Your Response

1. How can focusing on Christ help you to change?

2. How can you continue following "the truth you already have"?

LET THE TRUTH BE KNOWN

An honest personal inventory enhances our ability to change.

specially during World War II, Margaret Bourke-White distinguished herself as a photo-journalist and a woman who knew her destiny. In her autobiography decades later, Margaret attributed her sense of purpose to parents who taught and modeled a search for integrity. She wrote:

> I realize now how [my father's] entire purpose was focused toward attaining [a] self-set standard, how deep in him the philosophy was: never leave a job until you have done it to suit yourself and better than anyone else requires you to do it. Perhaps this unspoken creed was the most valuable inheritance a child could receive from her father.
>
> That, and the love of truth, which is requisite No. 1 for a photographer. And in this training Mother shared. When I was a very small child, if I broke a soup plate, Mother would say, "Margaret, was it an accident or was it carelessness?" If I said it was carelessness, I was punished; an accident, I was forgiven. I am proud

of Mother's vision in knowing how important it is to learn to be judge of one's own behavior. She did well to see that a habit of truth throughout life is more important than the broken soup plates. [13]

Margaret's personal evaluations later enabled her to cast a keen eye on the world. Whether photographing steel mills, migrant workers, German bombers, Joseph Stalin or Mahatma Gandhi, she courageously focused on detail and truth. With this approach, she broke the conventional bounds of photography and secured her place in history.

Margaret admittedly owed her success to an inner certainty since childhood. Her mother had told her, "Margaret, you can always be proud that you were invited into the world." [14]

*W*hat a wonderful legacy for a daughter—to know, for certain, that her parents wanted her birth and to feel secure and purposeful while growing up. Sadly, that's not the case for many children today.

But there's recompense.

Even if love and security aren't part of our earthly heritage, it certainly belongs to our heavenly legacy. God planned for each of us to visit the earth. Because He wants us. Because He loves us. And with that knowledge, we can bask in our relationship with Him and grow strong in our place in the world.

We can also honestly assess ourselves.

When we're loved deeply and unconditionally, there's safety in admitting our shortcomings and evaluating their impact. We can be truthful. We don't risk the humiliation of rejection. In fact, we long to change to please our loved one.

And so it can be with God.

When we grasp the Lord's magnanimous love for us, we no longer fear His recrimination for our sin and shortcomings. We repent with the sorrow of hurting a lover, but also with the certainty of His forgiveness. Openly assessing ourselves before God and confessing sin becomes the means for nurturing a precious relationship.

It also clears the path for change.

If the truth be known, there's a mystical link between honestly assessing ourselves and accomplishing real change. It's the link called repentance. When we repent of our sins, we gain the spiritual power and purity that can transform us.

The preacher Peter Marshall knew this, and in an oratory prayer, he told God:

> I dare to pray that something will happen to me in Thy presence. Lord, I know I need to be changed!
>
> Forgive me for all the intentions that were born and somehow never lived. These, Lord Jesus, are sins, grievous in Thy sight, grievous even in mine.
>
> And now I claim Thy promise to change me. Do thou for me what I cannot do for myself. Lead me into a new tomorrow with a new spirit. Cleanse my heart, create within me new attitudes and new ideas, as only Thou canst create them. [15]

May this be our prayer as we let the truth be known and begin to change.

❦

PERSONAL CHECKPOINT

1. Before God, have you honestly assessed yourself?

2. If not, what keeps you from telling Him the truth?

GOD'S VIEWPOINT

The psalmist confesses his sin to God:

> *Happy is the person*
> *whose sins are forgiven,*
> *whose wrongs are pardoned.*
> *Happy is the person*
> *whom the LORD does not consider guilty*
> *and in whom there is nothing false.*

When I kept things to myself,
I felt weak deep inside me.
I moaned all day long.
Then I confessed my sins to you
and didn't hide my guilt.
I said, "I will confess my sins to the LORD,"
and you forgave my guilt.

For this reason, all who obey you
should pray to you while they still can.
When troubles rise like a flood,
they will not reach them.
You are my hiding place.
You protect me from my troubles
and fill me with songs of salvation.

The LORD says, "I will make you wise and show you
where to go.
I will guide you and watch over you.
So don't be like a horse or donkey,
that doesn't understand.
They must be led with bits and reins,
or they will not come near you."

Wicked people have many troubles,
but the LORD's love surrounds those who trust him.
Good people, rejoice and be happy in the LORD.
Sing all you whose hearts are right.
—Psalm 32:1-3, 5-11

YOUR RESPONSE

1. How can you view God as a lover who will forgive you?

2. How might you honestly assess yourself before Him?

THE GIRL YOU LEFT BEHIND

Exploring childhood influences can help us understand our behaviors.

*I*n the early 1900s, Beryl Markham grew up with the sons of African warriors and tracked game with the best of them. As a young girl, she had moved with her parents from Great Britain to East Africa, against her genteel mother's protestations.

Africa suited Beryl. She identified with its wild and mysterious ways.

Her mother did not.

Clara missed her upper-class advantages and eventually sailed back to England without her husband and young daughter. It's speculated that Clara expected to return, so she left Beryl behind to enjoy the jungle instead of uprooting her once again. Whatever the intent, Clara later divorced her husband and never returned to Njoro where he and Beryl lived.

For this, Beryl never forgave her mother.

Several years later, Beryl's father retreated to Peru, driven to bankruptcy by the farm he and his daughter loved. Beryl had married not long before, but as a sixteen-year-old bride, she still wanted her father nearby and missed him dearly.

Based on first impressions, the abandonments didn't appear to mangle Beryl's life. She gained international fame as the first person to fly solo across the Atlantic Ocean from England to North America, against the headwinds. Before this, she had become Africa's first female thoroughbred trainer and its first woman bush pilot. She also published a best-selling book and numerous short stories about her adventures.

Personally, though, the desertions trailed Beryl for a lifetime. She never really liked women and seldom trusted men. She became notoriously promiscuous and harbored no conscience about how she spent money or if she paid mounting bills. It seemed that when Beryl's parents left, she abandoned her conscience and quested for attention. [16]

One can guess that Beryl didn't change her destructive habits since she never paused long enough to reckon with the childhood that shaped her womanhood. In her later years, when the fame had passed, she hated living alone with herself.

*M*uch of the goal to change personally centers on a struggle to live at peace with ourselves. If we stop the activity and sit quietly with ourselves, we would like to feel at ease with our own company.

Yet for many of us, that's when the agony begins. With time to think, we recount our sins and imperfections, fearing they may be discovered, or we worry about how they've already indicted us. It's much easier to keep busy and drown out the inner voice that nags us.

Strangely, it's this same voice of conscience that can lead us to peace—if we'll pause long enough to answer the questions and evaluate who we are and where we've been. It begins with reviewing our personal history and particularly the growing-up years.

With the experts and literature available today, most of us agree that childhood influences play a powerful role in shaping us. It takes considerable coaxing, though, to convince us to face the girl we've left behind. It can be too revealing and painful.

Who was she back then? How did life affect her? The answers to these and other questions point to the habits and attitudes we fight today. Understanding how our problems developed can help us to overcome them if we dare to act on the insights we gain.

But first, the questions. In regard to our need to change, we can begin with these:

Who modeled the attitudes that affect me today?

What were the less-than-desirable attitudes?

What problem behaviors run in my family?

Am I suffering from the "sins of my fathers"?

What hurt me as a child, a girl, a young woman?

How could this pain have molded my behavior?

What family patterns of relating shaped me?

What values were missing from my upbringing?

These are difficult questions. But they open the door for a hurting girl to face the past and turn into a woman without wounds.

PERSONAL CHECKPOINT

1. How do you feel about exploring your childhood for clues to your behavior today?

2. What could be the dangers and advantages of this exploration?

GOD'S VIEWPOINT

The Lord's promise to renew the past:

> The LORD says, "Forget what happened before,
>   and do not think about the past.
> Look at the new thing I am going to do.
>   It is already happening. Don't you see it?
> I will make a road in the desert
>   and rivers in the dry land."
>
> The LORD says, "People of Jacob,
>   you are my servants. Listen to me!
> People of Israel, I chose you."
> This is what the LORD says, who made you,
>   who formed you in your mother's body,
>   who will help you:

"People of Jacob, my servants, don't be afraid.
  Israel, I chose you.
I will pour out water for the thirsty land
  and make streams flow on dry land.
I will pour out my Spirit into your children
  and my blessing on your descendants.
Your children will grow like a tree in the grass,
  like poplar trees growing beside streams of water."

The Lord, the king of Israel,
  is the Lord All-Powerful, who saves Israel.
This is what he says: "I am the beginning and the end.
  I am the only God.
Who is a god like me?
  That god should come and prove it.
Let him tell and explain all that has happened since I
    set up my ancient people.
He should also tell what will happen in the future.
Don't be afraid! Don't worry!
  I have always told you what will happen.
You are my witnesses.
  There is no other God but me.
  I know of no other Rock; I am the only One."
                              —*Isaiah 43:18-19; 44:1-4, 6-8*

Your Response

1. If God says to "forget what happened before," should you care about understanding childhood influences?

2. At what point can you quit thinking about the past and look to the future?

GRABBING AT GRACE

**True change can begin when
we forgive ourselves of the past.**

hile my car's windshield wipers whapped at the sputtering rain, I glanced skyward and protested: *Oh, no, it can't rain. Not today; not now! Doesn't God realize how important these next few hours are?*

I pressed the gas pedal harder, urging the wipers and an aging engine to move ahead. And for the next half-hour we purposefully—almost defiantly—pulsed together: the wipers, the engine, the raindrops, my heart.

Uttering to their rhythm, I repeated my resolve: *I've got to get to the ocean. I've got to get to the ocean!* Because if I got there, somehow everything would be all right.

Finally at the beach, I quieted the car, rolled up my collar, and stepped into the drizzle. Then, while squishing along the shoreline, I pondered what I would soon dump into the gray waters.

About everything had gone wrong that year. And I had topped it all off with a fit of crankiness—downright rudeness—toward Mother when she visited me at Christmas time. Poor Mom. I had really unloaded on her, and my unhappiness wasn't her fault.

Now she had gone home, and I stumbled into the new year with a burden of remorse. To me, surliness toward Mom symbolized my sins and failures of that whole, horrible year. And no matter how hard I prayed, I couldn't cast off the accumulated guilt.

So driving to the ocean was my last shot at absolution—from the way I had treated my mother, from my piled-up failures, from my inability to change, from my reluctance to forgive myself. For some unexplainable reason, I felt compelled to return to the seaside spot where I had sniped at Mom the worst—and where water, a symbol of cleansing, flowed freely.

Pulling my coat closer, I mentally culled out nagging sins and failures, one by one. After I repented and asked God for forgiveness—and after I forgave myself—I imagined dumping each offense into the sea.

Then I whispered toward heaven, "Lord, I know Your love and forgiveness run deeper and wider than this ocean. So today I've repented, and now I'm accepting your absolution, once and for all. I'm throwing away this guilt, too!"

The next day my spirit lightened. And for weeks after, I recalled the "big dump" when I felt tempted to relive offenses I had discarded.

No, you can't pester me, I mentally said to lingering accusations. *I threw my guilt into the ocean on that rainy Sunday.*

Soon, even the temptation to feel guilty washed away, lost in the many waters of forgiveness.

When we reckon with our need to change, we can feel terrible remorse about how our behavior has harmed other people. But once we've asked them for forgiveness, the pardoning doesn't end there. It's equally important to forgive ourselves.

For women, this step can be difficult. Because of low self-esteem, family background, sensitivity, or emotional wounds, we often can't forgive ourselves. We repeatedly flog ourselves to prove true repentance, when in reality, we're refusing to grab God's grace.

We also stymie the change process. Until we forgive ourselves for who we've been, it's difficult to believe in who we can become.

The apostle Peter practiced self-forgiveness that opened the door to remarkable change. He cried bitterly after denying Jesus three times to protect himself from punishment (Matthew 26:69-75). Then when Jesus forgave him and said, "Feed my lambs," Peter rallied into a great spiritual leader (John 21:15).

At some point, Peter must have forgiven himself. He believed and fulfilled the prophecy that he would become the rock on which Christ could build the Church (Matthew 16:18). After Christ's ascension, Peter performed miracles and stood stalwart through persecution. But he couldn't have wielded such spiritual power while wallowing in unforgiveness.

Self-forgiveness needs exercise in many areas. It's necessary for absolving everyday mistakes and for life-changing failures. Yet if we truly repent, God will forgive any sin we've committed. So why shouldn't we forgive ourselves?

Each of us must probe that question. But really, there's only one answer. Just as we love Him because He first loved us, we also can forgive ourselves because He first forgave us. [17]

❧

PERSONAL CHECKPOINT

1. Have you forgiven yourself for the behavior you want to change?

2. What can be difficult about forgiving yourself?

GOD'S VIEWPOINT

The Lord's promise to His people:

> *"Look, the time is coming," says the LORD,*
> *"when I will make a new agreement*
> *with the people. . . .*
> *It will not be like the agreement*
> *I made with their ancestors*
> *when I took them by the hand*
> *to bring them out of Egypt.*

I was a husband to them,
    but they broke that agreement," says the Lord.
"I will put my teachings in their minds
    and write them on their hearts.
I will be their God,
    and they will be my people.
People will no longer have to teach their neighbors and
        relatives
    to know the Lord,
because all people will know me,
    from the least to the most important," says the Lord.
"I will forgive them for the wicked things they did,
    and I will not remember their sins anymore."

This is what the Lord says:
"Only if people can measure the sky above
    and learn the secrets of the earth below,
will I reject [my people]
    because of what they have done," says the Lord.
                    —Jeremiah 31:31-32, 33b-34, 37

YOUR RESPONSE

1. What causes you to reject and not forgive yourself?

2. How can you begin to model self-forgiveness after God's absolution of His people?

Part Three

WHEN THE INSIDE SPILLS OUT

Handling the pain and emotions of change

*I*n all our hearts, faith is mixed with doubt, love with bitterness. It is extremely difficult for us to acknowledge this utterly illogical and contradictory character of our feelings. It is true that the most contrary feelings can live side by side in our hearts: hope and despair, joy and sorrow, anxiety and trust. We are controlled by feelings, not by logic, though we fondly imagine that we are being guided by our reason. What happens in fact is that reason supplies the arguments with which to justify our behaviour. We appear to be logical, but are thoroughly illogical. That is one more contradiction. [18]

> Paul Tournier,
> *The Meaning of Persons*

*W*hen Angela decided to change, her friends felt the quake. For a year or two, she had suspected that something wasn't right—that perhaps a dysfunctional childhood had affected her adulthood behaviors. Plagued by insecurities and hyper-sensitivity, she routinely pushed friends and coworkers to the edge by questioning their motives and needing constant reassurance.

It took grit to be Angela's friend. She delighted us with warmth and humor and then clobbered us with accusations. Somehow, the good times outweighed the bad, and we stuck with her. (Not that we wore wings. We worked in the same office with Angela. We couldn't leave.)

Still, when Angela announced she had started therapy, we sighed with relief. She wanted to find peace for what churned inside her. We wanted that for Angela, too. We hoped for her best, never suspecting we would get the worst.

Nobody needed to ask Angela about her therapy appointments. Each morning after a session, she looked a wreck and acted even worse. On those mornings, she gloomily avoided us. Then gradually, for the next few days, her emotions spilled out as strong and unpredictable as our Midwest winters. It took about a week to get the "real" Angela back, but then the cycle began again.

We learned to hang on for the rumble.

As Angela worked through the grief of a tattered childhood, we watched her cry. When she confronted disappointments, we encountered her anger. As she pulled away from people pleasing, we got slammed by her assertiveness. When she wrestled with low self-esteem, we felt her shame.

About a year later, though, Angela's emotions began to subside. A warm and loving person showed up for work far more often than the insecure woman we had tolerated. Angela changed. She started to love the woman God created her to be. And so did we.

*A*ngela's story isn't unusual. When we begin to change, all kinds of emotions spill out, most of which we can't immediately control. Change uncorks what's bottled inside of us, and there's no predicting what's lurking within.

Also, Angela's emotions were necessary. Emotions help us sort out what needs to be changed. We can depend on them to guide us toward healing. They remind us of our humanity and our need for God. They signal that, yes, we've entered the change process.

Still, there's no excuse for pummeling people around us. (Angela was lucky we valued our jobs and paychecks, or we might not have stuck with her.) With the help of God's Word and His Spirit, we can gain insight to our emotions and gradually capture them before they torpedo everyone in sight. (And learn to request forgiveness when they do.)

So when we expect ourselves to change, we can anticipate the emotions, too. And when we hang on for the quake, more often than not, a lovable person will ascend from the debris.

Personal Checkpoint

In Part Three, explore the emotions common to the change process. But first, answer these questions:

1. What emotions have you felt in the change process?

2. How do you feel about your emotional reactions?

3. How might you learn to respond rather than react when your emotions spill?

A Stab in the Soul

God can fill the emptiness and disappointment of missed potential.

*I*n the 1950s, a young French man and woman sat on the left bank of the Seine River, weeping.

Why? Because they loved each other and couldn't express it. As students of philosopher Jean-Paul Sartre, they believed that the words "I love you" only meant "I have a sexual urge." Reductionist theories had taught them that love didn't exist—that it only disguised the animal instincts of procreation.

So the couple cried as they denied what they instinctively knew to be true: Love lives in the human heart. Denying its existence—and their potential as loving companions—stabbed their souls with confusion. [19]

*T*his year at the winter Olympic games, athletes from around the world competed for a chance to say they're the world's best. The games unfolded as a story of hope gained and lost.

It broke hearts when competitors, after years of strenuous training, lost the gold by inches or seconds or tenths of a point. Or when the unthinkable happened: A young girl fell from the balance beam; a sprinter stumbled to the ground and writhed in pain; a swimmer twice started falsely and got eliminated from a race.

For these Olympians, getting so close—and still losing—stabbed their souls with regret.

*N*ot long ago, I sat with a friend who, as of yet, hasn't overcome an addiction that's suffocating her sanity.

"When will I ever change?" she asked while sobbing. "I know I'm better than this!"

Now she doesn't want to keep trying to change. It's too hard. It's too discouraging. Constantly falling short of her expectations has stabbed her soul with pain.

A stab in the soul. That's how it feels when our behavior falls short and disappoints or even devastates us. We know we're capable of a better performance, but something blocks our potential. And usually that "something" dwells within us.

It's so frustrating.

It's also biblical. When God created the first man and woman in His image, He stamped them with His perfection. He never intended for humanity to suffer from flaws and incapability. But Adam and Eve's disobedience irrevocably changed us.

Ever after, we've lived with *the understanding* of perfection, but we've lacked *the ability* to achieve it. We succumb to weaknesses and sin. We long for the day when God will restore us to His ideal. (And sometimes, we mistakenly believe we can achieve it now.)

Even the earth groans with this expectation. "We know that everything God made has been waiting until now in pain, like a woman ready to give birth," wrote the apostle Paul to the Romans. "Not only the world, but we also have been waiting with pain inside us."

Then he reminded them of the good news.

"We have the Spirit as the first part of God's promise. So we are waiting for God to finish making us his own children, which means our bodies will be made free. Also, the Spirit helps us with our weaknesses," he explained (Romans 8:22-23, 26a).

After Jesus returned to heaven, God sent the Holy Spirit—the Comforter—to empower us for holy living. Not earthly perfection. Not everything we've always wanted. But to a higher level of living: a spiritual dimension that strengthens us for plodding a craggy and perilous world. And with the promise that, when we reach heaven, God will restore us to perfection.

In the meantime, we can reckon with our earth-bound limitations. With the Holy Spirit's help, we can change, but we'll never achieve perfection in these bodies or on this planet. Earthly transformations only serve as a deposit on heaven's matchless glories.

With this promise, He wants to stab our souls with joy.

PERSONAL CHECKPOINT

1. Is your soul stabbed with pain or joy? Why?

2. In your heart, do you long for perfection? How does this affect your change process?

GOD'S VIEWPOINT

On living in the Holy Spirit's power:

So now, those who are in Christ Jesus are not judged guilty. Through Christ Jesus the law of the Spirit that brings life made me free from the law that brings sin and death. The law was without power, because the law was made weak by our sinful selves. But God did what the law could not do. He sent his own Son to earth with the same human life that others use for sin. By sending his Son to be an offering to pay for sin, God used a human life to destroy sin. He did this so that we could be the kind of people the law correctly wants us to be. Now we do not live following our sinful selves, but we live following the Spirit.

Those who live following their sinful selves think only about things that their sinful selves want. But those who live following the Spirit are thinking about the things the Spirit wants them to do. If people's thinking is controlled by the sinful self, there is death. But if their thinking is con-

trolled by the Spirit, there is life and peace. When people's thinking is controlled by the sinful self, they are against God, because they refuse to obey God's law and really are not even able to obey God's law. Those people who are ruled by their sinful selves cannot please God.

But you are not ruled by your sinful selves. You are ruled by the Spirit, if that Spirit of God really lives in you. But the person who does not have the Spirit of Christ does not belong to Christ. Your body will always be dead because of sin. But if Christ is in you, then the Spirit gives you life, because Christ made you right with God. God raised Jesus from the dead, and if God's Spirit is living in you, he will also give life to your bodies that die. God is the One who raised Christ from the dead, and he will give life through his Spirit that lives in you.

So, my brothers and sisters, we must not be ruled by our sinful selves or live the way our sinful selves want. If you use your lives to do the wrong things your sinful selves want, you will die spiritually. But if you use the Spirit's help to stop doing the wrong things you do with your body, you will have true life.

—Romans 8:1-13

YOUR RESPONSE

1. How do your feel about your imperfection on earth?

2. How can you tap into the Spirit's power for holy living?

Day 12

LIVING IN LOUD DESPERATION

When used wisely, anger can facilitate the change process.

The mass of men lead lives of quiet desperation," said Henry Thoreau when he retreated to the woods and Walden Pond. [20]

Not so for everybody, says my friend Ellen.

"I live my life in loud desperation," she explains, referring to the incessant personal problems she's endured—and how vocal she's gotten about her pain and anger.

I love and respect that about Ellen. She's always honest about what she's thinking and feeling, even if it's difficult for her to say it.

I'm sure Ellen's therapist loves that about her, too. It's probably not necessary to coax out her feelings and opinions during a counseling session. I imagine they pull up chairs, seat themselves, and clamor for attention when the appointment begins. Faithfully, they've helped Ellen maneuver the change process.

A counselor once told me, "Since healing depends on honesty, it's much easier working with people who spill their emotions everywhere than spending weeks and months getting them to open up."

That counselor would have loved Ellen.

$\mathcal{L}$ike Ellen, many women exist comfortably—or at least knowingly—with their emotions. Although we're equally at home with our intellects, to touch us deeply is to respect and understand our feelings.

Still, there's one emotion that confuses us. We struggle with its expression and repress it. Or we let it rip and then feel humiliated. Ironically, men who're uneasy with emotion can express this feeling without thought. But as young girls, our mothers taught us to "be nice," so we fear its sound and fury.

We're uncomfortable with our anger.

"The taboos against our feeling and expressing anger are so powerful that even *knowing* when we are angry is not a simple matter. When a woman shows her anger, she is likely to be dismissed as irrational or worse," wrote psychologist Dr. Harriet Goldhor Lerner. "Thus, we . . . learn to fear our own anger, not only because it brings about the disapproval of others, but also because it signals the necessity for change." [21]

Yet, if we truly desire change, we need not fear our anger: It facilitates the transformation process. If used well, it can motivate us to begin changing and to keep persevering. Anger points to specific hurts and fights against what's wronged us. It desires wholeness and significance. It seeks justice. But anger can also demand revenge. For this reason, it helps to gauge whether it's healing rather than hurting, and motivating rather than destroying ourselves and others.

That's a leap for many of us. We're still at the stage where we repress anger and depress ourselves. Or we communicate it destructively and deepen the pain and bitterness. Or we displace it on the wrong things or people.

Or women like me combine all of these options and turn into a seething mess.

I remember one boss whose sparse compliments particularly bothered me. I would knock myself out on a project and he would barely notice—or point to small details that needed improvement. For months I felt depressed. Then I got angry, but instead of confronting him, I spewed on people around me.

One day while standing in my manager's office, waiting for his response to my work, my mind flashed back. Suddenly, I imagined myself as a fourth grader, standing in front of my father while he looked at my report card.

"Look, Dad," I reported. "I got straight A's this quarter."

"Yes, I see," he said, and handed it back to me.

My father's dismissal had crushed me. And standing in a corporate office, I realized my boss wasn't the root problem. I had transferred my need for fatherly approval to male superiors at work. I had displaced my anger and it nearly destroyed me.

Getting to the root of that anger helped me to understand, heal, and forgive. And that's how anger can work on our behalf: It can lead us toward forgiveness.

Ephesians 4:26 tells us to be angry, but not to sin. In other words, don't let anger lead to bitterness, unresolved conflict, and unforgiveness. That's far different than never getting angry at all. Anger is not a sin, but what we do with it can be.

As we work through the change process, the Holy Spirit can help us to discern the difference.

❦

PERSONAL CHECKPOINT

1. As you've worked toward change, have you felt angry? Why?

2. What could be at the root of your anger?

GOD'S VIEWPOINT

Paul writes about how to live:

You were taught to leave your old self—to stop living the evil way you lived before. The old self becomes worse, because people are fooled by the evil things they want to do. But you were taught to be made new in your hearts, to become a new person. That new person is made to be like God— made to be truly good and holy.

So you must stop telling lies. Tell each other the truth, because we all belong to each other in the same body. When you are angry, do not sin, and be sure to stop being angry before the end of the day. Do not give the devil a way to defeat you. Those who are stealing must stop stealing and start working. They should earn an honest living for themselves. Then they will have something to share with those who are poor.

When you talk, do not say harmful things, but say what people need—words that will help others become stronger. Then what you say will do good to those who listen to you. And do not make the Holy Spirit sad. The Spirit is God's proof that you belong to him. God gave you the Spirit to show that God will make you free when the final day comes. Do not be bitter or angry or mad. Never shout angrily or say things to hurt others. Never do anything evil. Be kind and loving to each other, and forgive each other just as God forgave you in Christ.

—Ephesians 4:22-32

Your Response

1. When Paul wrote, "Do not be bitter or angry or mad," do you think he meant never to express anger? Why, or why not?

2. How can you use anger to facilitate personal change?

HIDING FROM JOY

Christ can heal the humiliation of who we are and what we've done.

s long as she can remember, food played an important role in Maria's home life. Her parents loved to eat. To them, food symbolized family togetherness and their rich ethnic heritage.

So growing up, Maria didn't learn how to manage food—or realize that there's a limit to how much a person can eat before reaping the consequences.

"If you didn't eat second and third helpings, it offended my mother. She would think we didn't like her cooking and that she had failed at taking care of us, so we shoveled it in," explains Maria.

"Besides, my mom was a great cook," she adds with a weak smile.

Maria turned into a great cook, too. By age thirteen, she outweighed her friends but could outperform most women in her ability to create a mouth-watering feast.

"I was proud of my cooking ability. It gained my family's approval, and that bolstered my self-esteem," she says.

At school, however, the approval vanished.

"In my family, everyone was overweight, so I felt accepted. But especially in gym class at school, I noticed how much thinner the other girls were and I felt ashamed. We wore gym suits that revealed every lump, and I'll never forget the humiliation of taking group showers.

"Some girls made fun of my chubbiness. And that's when I took on shameful feelings about my body," she continues. "I suffered with it for years. Instead of changing myself, I went into hiding."

Maria "hid" by withdrawing at school, only participating when absolutely necessary and hanging out with the "misfits." As soon as possible, though, she returned to the comfort of home—and more food.

As the years progressed, she gained more weight and hid more often. "That is, as much as you could hide two hundred pounds," she adds.

"If I couldn't hide physically, I would at least hide mentally. It took years to realize that I wasn't just hiding my body. I was also hiding my shame. And until I uncovered my humiliation, I couldn't begin to accept myself and to change."

*S*hame is a powerful and perplexing force. Instead of propelling us toward change, it submerges us into the dark side of ourselves, alone and afraid of discovery.

"Shame's most important objective *is to not be exposed*," writes Stephanie E. in the recovery pamphlet, *Shame-Faced*. "Most people who are 'shame-based' don't know it. They can't. It's slippery.

"Sometimes it comes on so slowly, you won't know when you started to feel this way. And it is most often disguised as what it is *not:* irrational white rage, indifference, the overwhelming need to control, depression, confusion, flightiness, the obsession to use, numbness, panic, and the need to run. We will grasp whatever defense we can to survive slipping into the bottomless pit of shame." [22]

Unfortunately, these personal defenses don't eradicate the shame or help us change shame-based behaviors. And that's when we need the Gospel.

Since shame stands as a fundamental barrier to transformation, it captivated the core of Christ's mission on earth. Paul told the Hebrews: "Let us look only to Jesus, the One who began our faith and who makes it perfect. He suffered death on the cross. But *he accepted the shame* as if it were nothing because of the joy that God put before him" (Hebrews 12:2, emphasis added). When Jesus bore the punishment for sin, He also accepted the shame. So when we lay our sins at His feet, we can abandon our shame there, too.

When Christ forgives, He also heals. And the healing of shame releases us to change what binds us, if we replace hiding with persevering.

"Think about Jesus' example," Paul continued. "He held on while wicked people were doing evil things to him. So do not get tired and stop trying" (12:3). And do not hide from the joy He places before you.

❦

Personal Checkpoint

1. What shame do you hide within?

2. How does this shame keep you from changing?

God's Viewpoint

Isaiah foretold Christ's shame-bearing mission:

> *Who would have believed what we heard?*
> *Who saw the Lord's power in this?*
> *He grew up like a small plant before the Lord,*
> *like a root growing in a dry land.*
> *He had no special beauty or form to make us notice*
> *him;*
> *there was nothing in his appearance to make us*
> *desire him.*
> *He was hated and rejected by people.*

He had much pain and suffering.
People would not even look at him.
   He was hated, and we didn't even notice him.

But he took our suffering on him
   and felt our pain for us.
We saw his suffering
   and thought God was punishing him.
But he was wounded for the wrong we did;
   he was crushed for the evil we did.
The punishment, which made us well, was given to
   him,
   and we are healed because of his wounds.
We all have wandered away like sheep;
   each of us has gone his own way.
But the LORD has put on him the punishment
   for all the evil we have done.

But it was the LORD who decided
   to crush him and make him suffer.
   The LORD made his life a penalty offering,
but he will still see his descendants and live a long life.
   He will complete the things the LORD wants him to
   do.
"After his soul suffers many things,
   he will see life and be satisfied.
My good servant will make many people right with
   God;
   he will carry away their sins."
                    —Isaiah 53:1-6, 10-11

YOUR RESPONSE

1. How can you apply your understanding of God's forgiveness to your shame?

2. How might you begin to heal your shame?

WELCOME TO MY PITY PARTY

Feeling sorry for ourselves can delay personal change and destroy relationships.

I opened the gift and felt dumbfounded.

"Thanks for the stuffed animal," I finally said, turning over the gray donkey in my hands. I vaguely recognized him as Eeyore from the *Winnie-the-Pooh* stories.

Why in the world would she give this to me? I wondered after my friend left the office. *A donkey? Now really! I'm a grown woman.*

Still, whether or not my friend intended it, I sensed that Eeyore had arrived to deliver a message to me. *But what was it?* I set him aside and continued my work, but I couldn't cast off the curiosity.

Later when the nagging failed to subside, I bought a copy of A. A. Milne's classic book and found Eeyore in chapter six, feeling sorry for himself.

> Eeyore, the old grey Donkey, stood by the side of the stream, and looked at himself in the water.
>
> "Pathetic," he said. "That's what it is. Pathetic."
>
> He turned and walked slowly down the stream for twenty yards, splashed across it, and walked slowly

back on the other side. Then he looked at himself in the water again.

"As I thought," he said. "No better from *this* side. But nobody minds. Nobody cares. Pathetic, that's what it is."

There was a crackling noise in the bracken behind him, and out came Pooh.

"Good morning, Eeyore," said Pooh.

"Good morning, Pooh Bear," said Eeyore gloomily. "If it *is* a good morning," he said. "Which I doubt," said he.

"Why, what's the matter?"

"Nothing, Pooh Bear, nothing. We can't all, and some of us don't. That's all there is to it."

"Can't all *what?*" said Pooh, rubbing his nose.

"Gaiety. Song-and-dance. Here we go round the mulberry bush." [23]

Eeyore continued his lament and finally admitted that nobody had remembered his birthday. To compensate, the donkey threw a pity party by himself. Pooh Bear, in turn, tried to make the donkey happy.

The story struck an uneasy chord.

Lately, I had been feeling sorry for myself. Well, more like wallowing in self-pity. Life was tumbling and I had been grumbling through the days, blaming myself, pointing out my faults, and insisting things couldn't possibly get better. (I had even complained that some friends had forgotten my birthday!)

I had been a real Eeyore.

The simple story convicted me. And once again, God used an ass to speak to a stubborn child. (See Balaam and his donkey in Numbers 22:21-34.)

*S*elf-pity smacks with ugliness. It's demanding and self-obsessed. It saps our spirit and relationships. But it's tempting, particularly when deeply-rooted problems don't want to budge.

When there's proof that we're pathetic, it's a ripe time to grovel about ourselves. Instead, God wants us to give thanks. "Always be joyful. Pray continually, and give thanks whatever happens. That is what God wants for you in Christ Jesus. Do not hold back the work of the Holy Spirit," says 1 Thessalonians 5:16–19.

Give thanks? When we've got cellulite thighs, an untamed temper, a people-pleasing problem, or a drug addiction? When we eat too much, work too hard, and yell at the kids too many times?

Give thanks? That's what the Scripture says. As usual, God asks us to respond contrary to our inclinations. For that's when we release His power to change us attitudinally and experientially.

It's hard to comprehend. But so is our insistence on slogging through muddy bogs when we could dance in the high places with God. Maybe this simple slogan can help: Don't be an Eeyore when you could be a Pooh.

PERSONAL CHECKPOINT

1. Have you been an optimist or a pessimist about your need to change?

2. What's at the root of your self-pity?

GOD'S VIEWPOINT

Paul talks about the attitudes of believers:

Be full of joy in the Lord always. I will say again, be full of joy.

Let everyone see that you are gentle and kind. The Lord is coming soon. Do not worry about anything, but pray and ask God for everything you need, always giving thanks. And God's peace, which is so great we cannot understand it, will keep your hearts and minds in Christ Jesus.

Brothers and sisters, think about the things that are good and worthy of praise. Think about the things that are true and honorable and right and pure and beautiful and respected. Do what you learned and received from me, what I told you, and what you saw me do. And the God who gives peace will be with you.

Live in peace with each other. We ask you, brothers and sisters, to warn those who do not work. Encourage the people who are afraid. Help those who are weak. Be patient with everyone. Be sure that no one pays back wrong for wrong, but always try to do what is good for each other and for all people.

Always be joyful. Pray continually, and give thanks whatever happens. That is what God wants for you in Christ Jesus.

Do not hold back the work of the Holy Spirit. Do not treat prophecy as if it were unimportant. But test everything. Keep what is good, and stay away from everything that is evil.

Now may God himself, the God of peace, make you pure, belonging only to him. May your whole self—spirit, soul, and body—be kept safe and without fault when our Lord Jesus Christ comes. You can trust the One who calls you to do that for you.

—Philippians 4:4-9; 1 Thessalonians 5:13b-24

YOUR RESPONSE

1. How do you feel about thanking God for everything?

2. How could you begin?

Memories of Pandora

It's difficult to change without looking deep inside ourselves.

G reek mythology, in an effort to describe how evil entered the world, blamed women for it. Although they told several accounts of creation, the Greek storytellers agreed on these points: Men happily roamed the earth long before women entered it, and females instigated all of the unhappiness in this world.

One story said that the father of gods, Zeus, in anger toward the god Prometheus who cared more about humans than the gods, created a great evil toward men. She looked sweet and lovely and because of her great beauty, the gods gave her costly gifts. They called her Pandora, which meant "the gift of all." According to one historian, the Greeks said that "from her, the first woman, comes the race of women, who are evil to men, with a nature to do evil." [24]

Another story claimed that Pandora's curiosity, not her evil nature, created misfortune. The gods presented her with a box, but told her not to open it. She didn't know they each had placed something harmful in the container. So eventually, she gave in to her curiosity and opened it.

Out flew sickness, sorrow, and other misfortunes. Too late, Pandora tried shutting the lid. But fortunately, one compassionate god had placed hope in the box. And hope remains humanity's comfort while suffering.

*N*ow I adhere to the scriptural account of creation: I don't believe the Greek myths. They're merely a civilization's creative though misguided way of explaining life and its mysteries. But as someone who's working to alter personal behavior, I've thought about Pandora's box—and how it's a metaphor for the change process.

As a young girl in English class I read about Pandora's box. Even then I sensed that when we open up one problem area, there's more hiding beneath the surface. And that we're both curious and terrified to know what's inside certain "boxes" in life.

So memories of Pandora flooded back when I started opening up to change. Lifting the lid on low self-esteem unleashed a host of other problems, each terribly and painfully connected to the other. My crummy self-image related to my drive to perform, the way I spent money, a need to control, how much I ate, and . . . the list gets too humiliating to enumerate. I felt the evil within and wished I had never peeked inside.

Discovering that a "Pandora's box effect" was normal and essential to true change helped me to understand the process, but it didn't abolish the pain. Change requires that we open our inner selves and deal with what's below the surface—and that hurts. But strangely and gratefully, hope mingles with hurt.

"Although an inside look can be overwhelming (and indeed must be if the core direction of our life is to really shift), still there must be more to it than a journey into darkness," wrote psychologist Dr. Larry Crabb in his book *Inside Out*. He continued: "We are children of light. Even in the midst of darkness, we know where we're headed. We have a lamp that always reveals the next step and a hope that keeps us moving even when the lamp seems to go out." [25]

We can cling to and rely on that hope as we battle what's within. For where there is hope, there can be healing.

PERSONAL CHECKPOINT

1. How do you feel about looking inside yourself to change?

2. What, specifically, do you fear might be lurking inside?

GOD'S VIEWPOINT

A prayer for God's mercy:

> LORD, I am in great trouble,
>   so I call out to you.
> LORD, hear my voice;
>   listen to my prayer for help.
> LORD, if you punished people for all their sins,
>   no one would be left, Lord.
> But you forgive us,
>   so you are respected.
>
> I wait for the LORD to help me,
>   and I trust his word.
> I wait for the Lord to help me
>   more than night watchmen wait for the dawn,
>   more than night watchmen wait for the dawn.
>
> People of Israel, put your hope in the LORD
>   because he is loving
>   and able to save.
> He will save Israel
>   from all their sins.
>   —Psalm 130

YOUR RESPONSE

1. Does hope mingle with your hurt?

2. How can you cultivate hope as you look within yourself?

Part Four

STUMBLING
TOWARD FREEDOM

Surviving the ups and downs of transition

*N**o matter how crazy or self-defeating our current behavior appears to be, it exists for a reason and may serve a positive and protective function for ourselves or others. If we want to change, it is important to do so slowly so that we have the opportunity to observe and test out the impact of one small but significant change. . . . If we get ambitious and try to change too much too fast, we may not change at all. Instead, we may stir up so much anxiety and emotional intensity within ourselves and others as to eventually reinstate old patterns and behaviors. Or we may end up hastily cutting off from an important relationship, which is not necessarily a good solution.* [26]

Harriet Goldhor Lerner,
The Dance of Anger

ortysomething and single, Barbara skillfully managed people at the office. She was efficient, articulate, well-respected. Well, at least with her work. Barbara's relationship with her mother painted another picture.

When Mom called her at the office, Barbara sounded like a twelve-year-old girl, agreeing to every demand Mama made.

Leaving work each day, it got worse. Barbara still lived with her mother, a longtime widow and hypochondriac, and she waited on her mom's needs almost constantly. A behind-the-back joke at the office claimed Barbara and Mama would stay roomies until "death do them part."

Not oblivious to the joke, Barbara eventually took a lease on a condo by herself. She wanted to change her relationship with Mom.

However, the week Barbara moved in, her mother's phone calls increased. Soon Barbara had more responsibilities for her mother than before. She ran errands, cooked meals, even stayed overnight when Mom felt ill or lonely. Eventually, Barbara spent so much time with her mother that she decided to move back home.

"God wants me to care for my family," she explained to friends. "If I leave Mother, I'm showing a lack of honor."

People at work thought that Barbara lacked self-respect, and they noted her depression.

It's understandable that Barbara felt depressed. She had failed to survive a difficult transition, and consequently, her relationship with Mom never changed.

hen we set about to change ourselves or a situation, the transition seldom runs smoothly. We're exploring new territory, trying on new behaviors, shaking up well-ingrained patterns and making changes that other people might not appreciate. Surviving the ups and downs of the transition can be tough—and can last what feels like forever.

That's when we gain patience.

"My brothers and sisters, when you have many kinds of troubles, you should be full of joy, because you know that these troubles test your faith, and this will give you patience," wrote James to early Christians.

He continued: "Let your patience show itself perfectly in what you do. Then you will be perfect and complete and will have everything you need. But if any of you needs wisdom, you should ask God for it. He is generous and enjoys giving to all people, so he will give you wisdom" (James 1:2-5).

When we face the trials of transition, God can grant us the wisdom and patience to hang on. We can consider them a blessing because patience can lead to a remarkable, healing change that's worth the wait.

PERSONAL CHECKPOINT

In Part Four, you'll encounter the ups and downs of transition.

1. How are you surviving the difficulties of transition?

2. What tempts you to give up on changing?

3. How can you consider the trials of changing a joy?

DON'T JUST SAY IT

Confessing sin isn't enough.
God asks us to repent and change.

hen Rosalie's family sits down for an evening meal, an extravaganza begins. She spares no expense buying exotic food or cooking utensils to showcase her son's culinary abilities.

Of course, Rosalie spares no expense for anything. She sports designer clothes for herself, a state-of-the art computer for her daughter, an airplane for her husband, and whatever else she feels like charging to numerous credit cards and checking accounts.

An airplane? Well, maybe for a wealthy person's shopping list. But Rosalie isn't rich. She just spends lots of money, writes rubber checks, and never pays the bills. But somehow, she always manages to obtain more credit, more money, more things.

When her husband's paycheck advance isn't enough (and it never is), Rosalie alters the amount and cashes it at the bank. She empties her son's savings. When credit cards hit their maximum limits, she reports them as stolen so she doesn't have to pay the bills. When she wants even more spending power, she fakes her way into an enormous bank loan.

Rosalie maneuvers with such aplomb, she never gets caught or pays for her transgressions. She recognizes her sins, though. Rosalie regularly visits her town's tiny Catholic church. She confesses her activities to the priest, asks for absolution, receives his forgiveness, and trots out to exorbitantly spend money again.

"Catholicism is a wonderful religion," she tells a house guest one evening. "You admit your sins and they're not sins anymore."

Rosalie's crowning performance begins when, from her office at home, she cracks the computers at her daughter's workplace. First, Rosalie only alters the amount of her daughter's paycheck, but then she pirates money from the company's accounts.

All the while, she keeps confessing to the priest who, by now, comes unglued. The priest listens to her outrageous admissions, but because of the confessional booth's confidentiality, he can't tell anyone or turn Rosalie in to the authorities.

"It's not enough to confess everything," the priest warns Rosalie. "You have to be sorry. Truly sorry." She doesn't follow his advice.

Finally, when Rosalie tells the priest she's starting a multinational business to help people "beat the system" the way she does, he bangs his head against a wall and questions God after she leaves.

Sound unbelievable?

It is. Rosalie lives in the film, *Rosalie Goes Shopping*. Among other lessons, the movie points to the futility of a "faith" that doesn't transform us personally.

*I*n regard to confession, Rosalie got one thing right. She admitted her sins daily—and there's biblical precedence for talking to God that often.

In Psalm 5:3, David told the Lord, "Every morning you hear my voice. Every morning, I tell you what I need, and I wait for your answer." David interacted with God daily, making requests and listening for responses. However, he knew that if sin dwelt in his heart, the Lord would not hear him, so confession figured into those conversations, too (Psalm 66:18).

Still, that wasn't enough to please God.

Again in Psalm 5, David wrote: "You are not a God who is pleased with the wicked; you do not live with those who do evil. You destroy liars; the LORD hates those who kill and trick others"

(5:4, 6). And that's where Rosalie's confessions turned worthless. In the end, she didn't change because, in the beginning, she didn't intend to. She used confession to placate her conscience rather than to repent of her sins.

When we're working toward personal change, we can totter between feeling guilty about our sins and actually repenting of them. It's the latter that makes the difference to God and determines whether we truly change.

Instead of merely feeling regretful, repentance requires that we turn around and walk in a different direction, away from the sin that binds us. It doesn't mean we won't lose balance while turning and redirecting ourselves. Or that we won't stumble along the new path. It means that, with our will and God's supernatural power, we intend to stop doing evil and to please God.

PERSONAL CHECKPOINT

1. In the past, have you confessed your sin to ease your conscience or to repent and change?

2. After you confess sin, what keeps you from forsaking that sin and changing?

GOD'S VIEWPOINT

James explains the relationship of faith and behavior:

Faith that is alone—that does nothing—is dead.

Someone might say, "You have faith, but I have deeds." Show me your faith without doing anything, and I will show you my faith by what I do. You believe there is one God. Good! But the demons believe that, too, and they tremble with fear.

You foolish person! Must you be shown that faith that does nothing is worth nothing? Abraham, our ancestor, was made right with God by what he did when he offered his son Isaac on the altar. So you see that Abraham's faith and the things he did worked together. His faith was made perfect by what he did. This shows the full meaning of the Scripture that says: "Abraham believed God, and God accepted Abraham's faith, and that faith made him right with God." And Abraham was called God's friend. So you see that people are made right with God by what they do, not by faith only.

Another example is Rahab, a prostitute, who was made right with God by something she did. She welcomed the spies into her home and helped them escape by a different road.

Just as a person's body that does not have a spirit is dead, so faith that does nothing is dead!

—James 2:17b-26

YOUR RESPONSE

1. If faith that does nothing is dead, how alive is your faith right now?

2. In regard to change, how can you express your faith by your behavior?

Day

On the Habit of Uglification

Change is difficult enough, so don't imagine things worse than they are.

es, we went to school in the sea, though you mayn't believe it—"

"I never said I didn't!" interrupted Alice.

"You did," said the Mock Turtle.

"Hold your tongue!" added the Gryphon, before Alice could speak again. The Mock Turtle went on.

"We had the best of educations—in fact, we went to school every day—"

"*I've* been to a day-school, too," said Alice. "You needn't be so proud as all that."

"What extras?" asked the Mock Turtle, a little anxiously.

"Yes," said Alice, "we learned French and music."

"And washing?" said the Mock Turtle.

"Certainly not!" said Alice indignantly.

"Ah! Then yours wasn't a really good school," said the Mock Turtle, in a tone of great relief. "Now, at *ours,* they had, at the end of the bill, 'French, music, *and washing*—extra.'"

"You couldn't have wanted it much," said Alice, "living at the bottom of the sea."

"I couldn't afford to learn it," said the Mock Turtle with a sigh. "I only took the regular course."

"What was that?" enquired Alice.

"Reeling and Writhing, of course, to begin with," the Mock Turtle replied, "and then the different branches of Arithmetic—Ambition, Distraction, Uglification, and Derision."

"I never heard of 'Uglification,'" Alice ventured to say. "What is it?"

The Gyphron lifted up both its paws in surprise. "Never heard of uglifying!" it exclaimed. "You know what to beautify is, I suppose?"

"Yes," said Alice doubtfully, "it means—to—make—anything—prettier."

"Well, then," the Gryphon went on, "if you don't know what to uglify is, you *are* a simpleton." [27]

When Alice fell into Wonderland, she entered a world of fantasy and confusion. And evidently, a place where residents considered "uglification" an essential for living.

Alice never received the answer to her question about the meaning of uglification. But to continue the Gryphon's parallel, "to uglify" most likely means "to make things uglier." And I suspect that many of us, as it relates to ourselves, practice uglification regularly.

We're especially susceptible to uglification when we're trying to change. After we uncover a need to alter our behavior, we focus on what's wrong with ourselves to the point of distraction. Under a magnifying glass of scrutiny, we grow horrified with our undesirable features.

Uglifiers turn uncomfortable circumstances into untenable situations. When confronted with their need to change, they claim, "I can't believe I have this problem. . . . I don't do anything right. . . . I'm a horrible person!"

It's true that, to change, we need to face the truth about ourselves. (By now in this book, I've made that clear!) But there's a balance between accepting the truth and bludgeoning ourselves with it. Anything that's beaten up gets ugly, and if we constantly harangue about what's wrong with us, we'll deepen instead of heal our problems. Eventually, we can turn into the unmanageable woman whom we describe. It's an inevitable self-fulfilling prophecy, if not in reality, at least in our minds.

Consequently, in our mind's eye, we need to wrest the sledgehammer from our hands and replace it with a two-way mirror. On one side, we view ourselves as sinners in desperate need of grace; on the other side, we can choose to see ourselves through the eyes of God's acceptance, compassion, and forgiveness. And with His viewpoint, we can respect ourselves enough to change.

Amazing grace! how sweet the sound that saved a wretch like me! I once was lost, but now am found—was blind, but now I see. [28]

PERSONAL CHECKPOINT

1. Have you "uglified" your need to change? If so, how?

2. In your heart, have you grasped God's viewpoint of you?

GOD'S VIEWPOINT

Paul describes God's love for us:

He [Christ] is the One who created everything. His purpose was that through the church all the rulers and powers in the heavenly world will now know God's wisdom, which has so many forms. This agrees with the purpose God had since the beginning of time, and he carried out his plan through Christ Jesus our Lord. In Christ we can come before God with freedom and without fear. We can do this through faith in Christ. So I ask you not to become discouraged. . . .

I ask the Father in his great glory to give you the power to be strong inwardly through his Spirit. I pray that Christ will live in your hearts by faith and that your life will be strong in love and be built on love. And I pray that you and all God's holy people will have the power to understand the greatness of Christ's love—how wide and how long and how high and how deep that love is. Christ's love is greater than anyone can ever know, but I pray that you will be able to know that love. Then you can be filled with the fullness of God.

With God's power working in us, God can do much, much more than anything we can ask or imagine. To him be glory in the church and in Christ Jesus for all time, forever and ever.

—Ephesians 3:9b-13a, 16-21

YOUR RESPONSE

1. In your mind's eye, how wide, long, high, and deep is God's love for you?

2. When you're tempted to "uglify" yourself, how can you counter the accusations with God's love?

SOMEBODY PLEASE HELP ME!

God wants us to cry for help when we're overcome by ourselves.

uthor Andrew Morton confirmed to the world that royalty isn't what it's cracked up to be. His book about Princess Diana of England shattered the fairy-tale image of her marriage to Prince Charles.

According to Morton, early in their marriage Diana grew overwhelmed with the circumstances of her life: Three months pregnant with William, she suffered from morning sickness; she discovered that Charles nurtured a relationship with another woman; the constant media scrutiny exhausted her; the royal family's stilted lifestyle and social responsibilities intimidated and frustrated her. And until the pregnancy, she had suffered from frequent attacks of bulimia, a symptom of her troubled growing-up years.

Diana begged Charles to end his indifference toward her turmoil and to help.

After her first Christmas with the royal family, angry voices and sobbing emitted from the rooms occupied by the Prince and Princess of Wales. Diana pleaded with the prince for assistance and then threatened to take her life. He accused her of bluffing and prepared to ride his horse on the royal estate.

Troubled and determined, Diana promptly hurled herself down a long wooden staircase, endangering the life of their child. Charles, after discovering she and the baby survived without harm, went riding.

Several suicide incidents followed. Diana threw herself against a glass display cabinet. She slashed her wrists with a razor blade. She cut herself with the serrated edge of a lemon slicer. During an argument with Charles, she picked up a penknife and cut her chest and thighs.

Charles thought Diana faked her problems.

"They were desperate cries for help," Diana later told friends. These friends say that, for more than a decade of marriage, Charles has consistently ignored Diana's pleas. [29]

*W*hether or not we believe all of Morton's claims—or other stories written about the decayed royal marriage—it saddens me to think of anyone pleading for help and crashing against denial or indifference.

It happens more often than we might think.

One winter, my friend Carolyn embarked on a vacation to Hawaii with her extended family. Family members had saved money and looked forward to this trip, so above all, they wanted to enjoy it.

About two days into the vacation, though, Carolyn felt engulfed by deep, emotional pain. Living with her family again, years of unresolved hurt and shame surfaced toward them and turned her into a sobbing heap.

"I felt shocked and humiliated, to say the least," she told me. "I had no idea the hurt was there, that it would surface, and that I couldn't control it. That was the worst part—that I couldn't push it back inside of me. I thought I was ruining everybody's big vacation."

Her family did, too. After Carolyn explained the sobbing to her mom and sister, they backed off. For the rest of the week, the family left Carolyn alone in the cabin, crying, while they took day trips. Nobody else asked about her sorrow.

When we feel desperate in our need to change, we can turn manic in our cries for help. This urgent need for help can occur any time during the change process: when we begin to change, after we've tried and failed, or when we need endurance for the long, last haul. And its desperation can shock, confuse, and humiliate ourselves and those around us.

Unfortunately, we don't always receive help from the people who could touch us most deeply.

It's tempting to shut down and turn inward from this rejection, but it's crucial that we do not. When we cry for help, we're near a turning point that could eventually heal us. If we don't keep moving forward, we could fall deeper into our destructive behaviors.

So when we're rejected by those who won't listen, we can remember that somewhere—in a home, in a church, in a psychologist's office—there are people who will hear us and respond. And we need to keep crying out until we find them.

It takes courage: the kind that states our needs without hysterically slashing our wrists.

We can find that courage in God, who wants us to cry out to Him, day or night, and as often as we need to. He never tires of listening to us, of helping us, of creating miracles that heal our hearts and change us.

When others reject us, the Lord lingers on. His Spirit will never leave or forsake us, until the day we meet Him face-to-face in heaven, crying with joy.

❦

PERSONAL CHECKPOINT

1. Has anyone rejected your cries for help? If so, how did you feel?

2. When you're rejected, what are you tempted to do?

GOD'S VIEWPOINT

David cries out to God for help:

I cry out to the LORD;
    I pray to the LORD for mercy.
I pour out my problems to him;
    I tell him my troubles.
When I am afraid,
    you, LORD, know the way out.
In the path where I walk,
    a trap is hidden for me.
Look around me and see.
    No one cares about me.
I have no place of safety;
    no one cares if I live.

LORD, I cry out to you.
    I say, "You are my protection.
    You are all I want in this life."
Listen to my cry,
    because I am helpless.
Save me from those who are chasing me,
    because they are too strong for me.
Free me from my prison,
    and then I will praise your name.
Then good people will surround me,
    because you have taken care of me.
                —Psalm 142

YOUR RESPONSE

1. How can you learn to cry out to God with your pain?

2. How do you want Him to respond?

TWO STEPS FORWARD, FORTY STEPS BACK

Setbacks can strengthen our motivation to change.

I have probably read *House and Garden* and *Metropolitan Home* for too long, so maybe my expectations have grown too big. But this summer, I created ambitious plans for remodeling the yard and pushed myself toward them.

When I moved into this house a year ago, it reminded me of a cross between a jungle and a desert. While weeds and spindly perennials strangled the yard's outer edges, parched and barren brown spots filled the lawn. In the truest sense of the words, the yard qualified as a natural disaster. I knew it would take work to restore the property to its original beauty, and a friend suggested that I get help.

Except for one rototilling and tree-pulling Saturday in March, I ignored the suggestion.

In her book *Green Thoughts,* the writer/gardener Eleanor Perényi had told me: "Well-trained gardeners who like their work must live [somewhere] in America, but not around here and not in my price range. When I look back on the long procession of . . . eccentrics, young and old, foreign and domestic, who have worked for me, I wonder how I and the garden have survived their ministrations." [30]

She then described numerous hired workers who had regressed or ruined her gardens.

None of that for me. I decided to shoulder the work myself, despite a weak back and a book deadline. I pulled up weeds, hacked back vines, transplanted grass, dug out flowerbeds, hauled around compost, erected a small greenhouse, inset stone edgings and paths, haunted the nurseries, planted a few hundred flowers, initiated an herb garden, poured out red bark, smelled up my car with sheep manure, conducted a mulch marathon, and set out planted terra-cotta pots and window boxes.

The potential beauty motivated me, but so did two approaching events. I had accepted an invitation to speak at a writer's conference in mid June and wanted to complete the yard work by that time. Then the flowers could grow lush for a future business commitment, a backyard barbecue in July.

I finished the yard. I attended the conference. And while I was gone, a hailstorm shredded my gardens. With nary a blossom in sight—and plenty of debris in the yard—the setback felt like starting all over again. With a compassionate friend and an attack of the blues, I spent a day cleaning up the yard.

Ironically, the barbecue that had pushed me to finish planting got canceled. All that work, all that stress, for a devastated yard with nothing to show off. It felt as though I had taken two steps forward, only to fall forty steps back.

*I*t's September now, and looking out my home's office window, it's hard to imagine why I felt upset. In the gardens, flowers bend with blossoms and herbs escape the boundaries of their bed. With food, water, and some pruning, nature recovered from itself.

In addition to the hail, the yard also survived several bouts with bugs, too much rain, not enough sun, and too many chilly nights. The garden's resiliency amazes me.

Thinking about the yard's comeback, I remind myself that personal change experiences setbacks, too. In the garden and in life, nothing grows in a straight line. But we can train and nurture the unwieldy growth—and confront the bugs, drought, and storms that rail against it—until someday, with luscious curves and color, it rebounds and blooms.

Accordingly, we can view personal setbacks as temporary challenges rather than permanent defeats. Even when winter settles in, there's always the promise of spring growth, if we're willing to cultivate again. Infused by the Holy Spirit, the human soul can stay amazingly resilient.

So whatever the mistake, whatever the falling back into sin, we can depend on God to forgive us and help us restart. We needn't give up our hope to change.

He has promised: "I will make up to you for the years that the swarming locust has eaten . . . and you shall have plenty to eat and be satisfied, and praise the name of the LORD your God, who has dealt wondrously with you; then My people will never be put to shame" (Joel 2:25-26; NASB).

After a summer of killing bugs, I can attest to the profundity of that promise.

PERSONAL CHECKPOINT

1. What has set you back from changing?

2. How did this setback happen?

GOD'S VIEWPOINT

God's free offer of mercy to us:

> The LORD says, "All you who are thirsty,
>   come and drink.
> Those of you who do not have money,
>   come, buy and eat!
> Come buy wine and milk
>   without money and without cost.
> Why spend your money on something that is not real
>   food?
>   Why work for something that doesn't really satisfy
>   you?

Listen closely to me, and you will eat what is good;
  your soul will enjoy the rich food that satisfies.
Come to me and listen;
  listen to me so you may live.
I will make an agreement with you that will last
    forever.
  I will give you the blessings I promised to David."

So you should look for the LORD before it is too late;
  you should call to him while he is near.
The wicked should stop doing wrong,
  and they should stop their evil thoughts.
They should return to the LORD so he
    may have mercy on them.
  They should come to our God, because
    he will freely forgive them.

"So you will go out with joy
  and be led out in peace.
The mountains and hills will burst into song before
    you,
  and all the tress in the fields will clap their hands.
Large cypress trees will grow where thornbushes were.
  Myrtle trees will grow where weeds were.
These things will be a reminder of the LORD's promise,
  and this reminder will never be destroyed."
                                    —Isaiah 55:1-3, 6-7, 12-13

YOUR RESPONSE

1. How can you recover from a setback?

2. How can you begin again to change?

THE PARALYSIS OF ANALYSIS

Too much information without experience stagnates our ability to change.

*M*eet Becky. She's heir to a difficult childhood and plenty to work through as an adult. People who know Becky can't help but admire her willingness to honestly evaluate herself and to face personal problems.

Becky visits a counselor regularly. She's an avid reader and serves as a walking encyclopedia on personal addictions and dysfunctions. With this knowledge, she frequently counsels friends who struggle with themselves and want to change. They look to Becky for comfort and wisdom.

Like many of us, though, Becky suffers from a fatal flaw. She knows what's wrong with herself, inside and out. But she never changes. She's stuck in the paralysis of analysis.

*I*t sounds strange, but it's possible to amass so much information that it stifles our ability to change. We lose our spontaneity, our capability to decide, our willingness to risk, our desire to wade into the depths with God. Too much information and self-evaluation can blind our faith—and it's faith that unleashes God's supernatural power to change us.

The practical theologian A.W. Tozer wrote about the need to add faith to our knowledge:

> There is knowledge beyond and above that furnished by observation; it is knowledge received by faith. . . . Divine revelation through the inspired Scriptures offers data which lie altogether outside of and above the power of the mind to discover.
>
> The mind can make its deductions after it has received these data by faith, but it cannot find them by itself. . . . If we ever come to know these things it must be by receiving as true a body of doctrine which we have no way of verifying. This is the knowledge of faith.
>
> There is yet a purer knowledge than this; it is knowledge by direct spiritual experience. About it there is an immediacy that places it beyond doubt. Since it was not acquired by reason operating on intellectual data, the possibility of error is eliminated. Through the indwelling Spirit the human spirit is brought into immediate contact with higher spiritual reality. It looks upon, tastes, feels and sees the powers of the world to come and has a conscious encounter with God invisible.
>
> Let it be understood that such knowledge is experienced rather than acquired. [A person] knows God in the last irreducible meaning of the word *know*. It may almost be said that *God happened to him.* [31]

Tozer aptly coined it. Unless we let God "happen to us," we can't truly know Him. And without experiencing Him, we'll miss out on deep, personal change.

But how do we let God happen to us?

Author Karen Burton Mains explained that when many people ask this question, they "don't particularly want a sincere answer; they want some sort of intellectual hocus-pocus, some kind of theorizing that sounds mystical and otherworldly.

"So the most offensive answer to give these people is: 'Read your Bible and pray, and ask for the Holy Spirit to teach you'

. . . In their hearts, they already know what to do. . . . It is often simply doing the things we already know to do." [32]

James told the early Christians, "Come near to God, and God will come near to you" (James 4:8). When we consistently and persistently draw close to God, He happens to us. Contrary to popular belief, a life-changing relationship requires that we spend both *quality* and *quantity* of time with the other person. It's also true with God.

I know it sounds simple, but think about it: If we spent as much or more time with God, asking Him to change us, as we do with our books and support groups about change, a miracle could happen.

God might actually change us.

I'm not advocating that we abandon books, counselors, and support groups but that we avoid substituting them for God and His supernatural power. When we sit with God, we soak in His character and gather up the faith to leap into His mystical resources. We begin to believe and trust that He can change us, rather than depending on mere mortals. We know Him well enough to ask for the miraculous.

When we draw close to God, we eventually begin to experience rather than just accumulate knowledge. And we're gradually set free from the paralysis of analysis.

PERSONAL CHECKPOINT

1. Are you caught in the paralysis of analysis?

2. Do you *experientially* believe in God's supernatural power to change you?

GOD'S VIEWPOINT

About drawing near to God:

God's word is alive and working and is sharper than a double-edged sword. It cuts all the way into us, where the soul and the spirit are joined, to the center of our joints and bones. And it judges the thoughts and feelings in our hearts. Nothing in all the world can be hidden from God. Everything is clear and lies open before him, and to him we must explain the way we have lived.

Since we have a great high priest, Jesus the Son of God, who has gone into heaven, let us hold on to the faith we have. For our high priest is able to understand our weaknesses. When he lived on earth, he was tempted in every way that we are, but he did not sin. Let us, then, feel very sure that we can come before God's throne where there is grace. There we can receive mercy and grace to help us when we need it.

—Hebrews 4:12-16

So give yourselves completely to God. Stand against the devil, and the devil will run from you. Come near to God, and God will come near to you.

—James 4:7-8a

YOUR RESPONSE

1. What keeps you from drawing close to God?

2. How can you draw near to Him?

Part Five

SMARTER, NOT HARDER

Fighting small battles for big gains

*piritual warfare in any of its victories is achieved
through objective fact and not through subjective feelings. War against our flesh must proceed on the basis of truth
and the appropriation of truth, and not on the untrustworthy
basis of feeling. [So] as believers we are to aggressively act in
taking the armor [of God] and putting it on. Every time we
face the enemy and battle him we should be sure our armor is
in place. Daily we need to appropriate our provided armor
and put on our spiritual dress for battle. A very close, hard-
fought battle is always before us. Facing that battle without
armor is unthinkable.* [33]

Mark I. Bubeck,
The Adversary

*L*ast July, I learned about car maintenance the hard way. It wasn't that I didn't know anything about cars. Or that I didn't know anything about *my* car. After all, I've driven my Ford Escort for ten years and intimately know every snort and chortle she throws at the road. We've survived many trips and tune-ups together. In fact, my car has stuck by me longer than some friendships, most commitments, and all of my jobs.

We've grown attached to each other. I put up with her quirks and she forgives mine. So when friends jab me with car jokes, I shrug them off. The long-suffering "E" has been good to me. I won't betray an automobile that's blessed me with years of no car payments and moderate repairs.

Besides, my brother-in-law once kept a car running for twenty-five years. He probably set a record for people who don't deal in antiques, and when I think of that old station wagon, the Escort's dents don't look so bad.

But let me clarify. My brother-in-law kept that automobile going because he's frugal. That's hardly a description of me. I keep pushing the Escort's endurance so I can buy furniture for my house. Despite our different motivations, the inspiration of Larry's old car helps "E" escape the used car lots. And she's probably grateful for that. It's tough breaking up a long-term relationship.

That's why, among other reasons, this summer's episode felt so traumatic.

In retrospect, I recognize that "E" had been sending signals to me about an ailment for several months. I ignored them because the symptoms didn't seem significant enough and I didn't want to spend the money—at least not on car repairs. (In my defense, I must say that the car's red "Engine" light never turned on, but that's still no excuse for denying her increasing pleas.)

Finally, when she could stand it no longer, "E" cracked her engine and with smoke billowing from under the hood, she stranded us on the highway and racked up an $1,800 repair bill. Her radiator fluid had drained out—a simple and relatively inexpensive repair if I'd heeded her warnings.

E sits in the driveway this morning, content with new valves and apologetic that she left me for three weeks and cost so much money.

I'm sorry, too. Sorry that sometimes I don't wake up until a problem grows enormous—sorry that when I don't confront small incidents, I'm forced into big, unnecessary traumas that grind my life to a halt until they're solved.

So I'm trying to remember that about change.

If I pay attention and fight the small battles, in the end, I'll win the war. That's especially true in the spiritual realm. Daily decisions can turn into big gains or losses.

It's up to me to choose.

PERSONAL CHECKPOINT

In Part Five, you'll learn about daily choices that make a difference in whether or not you change.

1. What critical, daily choices do you face in your desire to change?

2. How can you learn to make choices that lead to positive change?

3. How can you know if you're making the right choices?

CHOOSE IT
OR LOSE IT

God's Word helps us to make choices that change us.

I live in the land of weekend warriors.

On Friday afternoons in Colorado, otherwise reasonable office people gear up to risk their lives on the mountains. In the winter, it's skiing down steep slopes or racing a snowmobile. In the summer, it's scrambling up craggy rocks toward the peaks, biking the narrow trails, or rafting down white-water rapids.

Whether they're parading up or down our hills, these warriors want to conquer the mountains with speed and physical prowess. However, it's not really the weekend that separates conditioned athletes from the dabblers. Monday morning does that.

Sliding back into their desks, the bodies of weekend athletes revolt with aches and pains. The people who stay perpetually conditioned feel great. (I solve the problem by not approaching the mountains at all, but the pain hits me after a weekend of stooping over flowerbeds.)

Still, the suffering could be avoided if we weekenders would take small steps toward conditioning instead of big jumps into muscle misery.

According to one doctor of orthopedics, "Failure to condition is the main reason why the weekend athlete suffers so much soreness and so many injuries." In an interview, he described the weekend athlete as a thirty-five-year-old businessman or woman who wants to recapture youth by getting back into shape.

"But they were never taught in school what getting back into shape meant, so they don't know how to properly go about it," he added.

It narrows down to flexibility.

"They have to stretch their muscles," he cautioned. "Muscles contract and expand. If you spend fifteen years without contracting and expanding them, and then suddenly begin contracting them by playing sports, the muscles will pull apart."

Ouch.

Ironically, it doesn't require much to get muscles into shape. The doctor recommended "a few basic stretching and limbering exercises, done regularly and right before athletic activity . . . to keep a person tuned up." [34]

*I*n the spiritual as well as the physical world, it's necessary to "choose it or lose it" to stay in shape. If we don't stretch our spiritual muscles regularly, they won't hold up under the strain of daily stresses, let alone the tribulations of working through change.

Part of this spiritual workout includes reading God's Word, the Bible.

In his book *My Friend, the Bible,* John Sherrill described his personal quest to understand and apply the Scriptures to his daily life. As he spent more time in the Bible, he discovered two kinds of verses that infuse God's "mystic energy" into our souls and keep us flexible for each day's challenges.

• **Manna verses** speak to us daily. God quickens our spirits as we read these Scriptures, and often they apply immediately to day-to-day living. Sherrill said these verses "emphasize the oddly elusive nature of our relationship with God. We need to come to Him daily for a new supply of Himself. We can't capture Him, box Him."

• **Arsenal verses** emphasize the opposite principle. Through memorization, meditation, and recall, these verses store up in our brains for a time when we need them. At the right moment, they march through our thoughts to guide our actions. "God's Word is also imperishable, inexhaustible, eternal," explained Sherrill, "and it can be stored up just as swords can be stored in an arsenal." [35]

In the spiritual realm, we can't afford to be weekend warriors. We need the daily manna and the stored-up arsenal to gather our strength and flexibility for battle. With both types of Scriptures prompting us, we can choose and not lose our quest for personal change.

PERSONAL CHECKPOINT

1. As you seek to change, how can you keep your spiritual muscles flexible?

2. Are you allowing God's Word to guide you through the change process?

GOD'S VIEWPOINT

God's Word guides the psalmist:

> *Happy are those who live pure lives,*
> *who follow the LORD's teachings.*
> *Happy are those who keep his rules,*
> *who try to obey him with their whole heart.*
> *They don't do what is wrong;*
> *they follow his ways.*
> *LORD, you gave your orders*
> *to be obeyed completely.*
> *I wish I were more loyal*
> *in obeying your demands.*
> *Then I would not be ashamed*
> *when I study your commands.*
> *When I learned that your laws are fair,*

I praised you with an honest heart.
I will obey your demands,
so please don't ever leave me.

How can a young person live a pure life?
By obeying your word.
With all my heart I try to obey you.
Don't let me break your commands.
I have taken your words to heart
so I would not sin against you.
LORD, you should be praised.
Teach me your demands.
My lips will tell about
all the laws you have spoken.
I enjoy living by your rules
as people enjoy great riches.
I think about your orders
and study your ways.
I enjoy obeying your demands,
and I will not forget your word.

—Psalm 119:1-16

YOUR RESPONSE

1. How and when can you gather up manna verses for daily living?

2. To help you change, what Scriptures might you add to your collection of arsenal verses?

Good-bye, Damsel in Distress

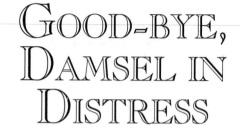

Change means letting go of a rescue mentality and accepting responsibility.

We're as helpless as we think we are.

That's what researchers concluded when they studied adolescents and their orientation toward intelligence and challenge. They studied the behavior of middle and junior high students and discovered two basic but opposite responses to difficulty or challenge: the "mastery" and the "helpless" patterns.

"In the helpless pattern, children seem[ed] trapped by the experience of difficulty, attributing it to a lack of intelligence," said the research report. Even if they had proved their ability in other areas, they often said, "I'm not smart at this." They felt upset about pressure, slackened their efforts, and lost sight of their objectives.

These students "believe[d] that intelligence is something they cannot change and that failure is an indictment of their ability," the report continued.

In contrast, mastery-oriented students "seem[ed] to believe they can become more intelligent through effort." They used effective problem-solving strategies and felt "excited and spurred by difficulty rather than threatened or anxious."

As a result, intelligence played a small part in these students' success at school. Even with "average" intelligence, the mastery-oriented students achieved much higher grades than their highly intelligent but helpless-oriented peers. [36]

And herein lies another lesson for the change-oriented person. If we believe we can change, we're prone to accomplish it. If we doubt our ability to change, we're positioning ourselves for failure.

*B*ut how do we believe in our ability to change?

It begins with dropping our damsel-in-distress mentality—the belief by women that another person will rescue us and accomplish the task for us. It's not ungodly or unfeminine to accept responsibility for ourselves. In fact, the Bible says that each of us will account for how we've managed our lives (Romans 14:10–12).

I don't mean to sound harsh, but from my experience, it's the helpless pattern that most often blocks women from their dreams. And nobody can change that pattern, except us. Parents can rescue us from a bad financial situation, but they can't change our inner attitudes about money. A diet counselor can cheer us on, but he can't lose the weight for us. A psychologist can listen to our problems each week, but she won't make our day-to-day decisions for us. It's up to us to believe, to work, to move toward change.

And then it's up to God.

Somebody once said we should work as though everything depended on us and pray as though everything depended on God. This admonition has turned into a cliché, and that's the risk of words that ring both profound and practical: They're quoted so many times they turn meaningless. But that doesn't negate the truth about work and prayer, our part and especially God's part. His promises and character never change.

Simply put, change begins with taking responsibility for ourselves and proceeds with depending on God. We become mastery-oriented because we step out and trust the Master who desires what's best for us.

❧

PERSONAL CHECKPOINT

1. Do you harbor a rescue mentality about your need to change?

2. How do you feel about taking responsibility for changing yourself?

GOD'S VIEWPOINT

What God has already done to help us:

> *It is written in the Scriptures:*
> *"'As surely as I live,' says the Lord,*
> *'Everyone will bow before me;*
> *everyone will say that I am God.'"*
> *So each of us will have to answer to God.*
>
> *[But] since we have been made right with God by our faith, we have peace with God. This happened through our Lord Jesus Christ, who has brought us into that blessing of God's grace that we now enjoy. And we are happy because of the hope we have of sharing God's glory. We also have joy with our troubles, because we know that these troubles produce patience. And patience produces character, and character produces hope. And this hope will never disappoint us, because God has poured out his love to fill our hearts. He gave us his love through the Holy Spirit, whom God has given to us.*
>
> *When we were unable to help ourselves, at the moment of our need, Christ died for us, although we were living against God. Very few people will die to save the life of someone else. Although perhaps for a good person someone might possibly die. But God shows his great love for us in this way: Christ died for us while we were still sinners.*
>
> *So through Christ we will surely be saved from God's anger, because we have been made right with God by the blood of Christ's death.*
> *—Romans 14:11-12; 5:1-9*

Your Response

1. How can you balance between taking responsibility for yourself and trusting God to help you?

2. What do you need to take responsibility for now?

The Woman
You'll Never Be

**A healthy outlook emerges when we
grieve and accept what can't change.**

You know, I thought I'd be famous by now," said Jeane who soon would turn thirty.

"What?" someone in our group sputtered.

"Well, I always thought I'd be well known for something I do. And I thought I had to do it by thirty," she explained. Then she asked us, "Didn't you think you'd be famous?"

Nervous laughter passed through the room.

Well, yes, some of us did. In fact, three out of five of us had thought that.

"My husband and I thought we'd be famous together," ventured an art director who's married to a photographer.

"I thought I'd be a famous writer," I said. Then I joked, "Well, at least I'm a writer."

"I guess growing older means coming to grips with who you really are instead of who you thought you would be," said Jeane.

"I guess there are some things we aren't destined to be," I added reluctantly.

It's true. Because of genetics or destiny or circumstances, there are some things we'll never achieve. And no amount of grit or hope or prayer will change us. Maybe if my coworkers and I had tried harder, we might have been famous by now. But we can't change the fact that one is Asian, one is tall, and one is thin no matter how much she eats.

There are some things we'll never change. But despite the facts, we still try to change them.

Take body image, for example. Recent ground-breaking research revealed that "fashion models have an abnormal body configuration that no amount of dieting will allow a normal woman to match." The bodies that we crave and diet for can't be ours, unless we're born with abnormal genes or turn anorexic. In fact, "fashion models are actually *less* at risk for eating disorders like anorexia and bulimia than normal women." [37]

Not long ago, the *Good Morning America* show reported that the average woman is 5' 3" tall and weighs 144 pounds. I've heard other reports that this average woman wears a size twelve.

So why the fuss to achieve a size six body?

Even without meaning to, we can listen to the world instead of to God.

So to be sure we're hearing His voice and pursuing the right objectives, we need checkpoints along our journey to change. We can ask God to confirm our direction, and if He says we're trying to alter what can't be changed, it's time to listen up. With God all things are possible, but some things He leaves as is.

We don't have to take the news with a stiff upper lip, though. In fact, it's healthy to grieve what we can't change. The anger, the depression, the bargaining helps us to finally accept what's inevitable and to productively proceed with life—and to focus on changing what actually *can* be changed. We're also assured that God's love and grace will hover over us and heal our grief.

Why am I introducing this now? Why not at the beginning of the book? Maybe I'm judging by my own hard-headedness, but it often takes time and failure to accept what's realistic and what's not.

God, give us grace to accept with serenity the things that cannot be changed, courage to change the things which should be changed, and the wisdom to distinguish the one from the other. [38]

PERSONAL CHECKPOINT

1. Could you be trying to change what can't be changed?

2. How do you feel about this as a possibility?

GOD'S VIEWPOINT

Help for when we don't know what to do:

The Spirit helps us with our weakness. We do not know how to pray as we should. But the Spirit himself speaks to God for us, even begs God for us with deep feelings that words cannot explain. God can see what is in people's hearts. And he knows what is in the mind of the Spirit, because the Spirit speaks to God for his people in the way God wants.

We know that in everything God works for the good of those who love him. They are the people he called, because that was his plan.

So what should we say about this? If God is with us, no one can defeat us. He did not spare his own Son but gave him for us all. So with Jesus, God will surely give us all things. Can anything separate us from the love Christ has for us? Can troubles or problems or sufferings or hunger or nakedness or danger or violent death?

But in all these things we have full victory through God who showed his love for us. Yes, I am sure that neither death, nor life, nor angels, nor ruling spirits, nothing now, nothing in the future, no powers, nothing above us, nothing below us, nor anything else in the whole world will ever be able to separate us from the love of God that is in Christ Jesus our Lord.

—*Romans 8:26-28, 31-32, 35, 37-39*

YOUR RESPONSE

1. In regard to personal change, how might you confirm God's direction for you?

2. Are you willing to grieve the things that can't be changed? Why, or why not?

WHO NEEDS REASONABLE?

When we quest for significant change, vision matters more than acceptance.

hen Georgia O'Keefe exhibited paintings in New York, critics misunderstood her art's intent.

"The things they write sound so strange and far removed from what I feel of myself," she wrote in 1922. In response, she set about defining herself and her work. Not to answer the critics, but to clarify and understand her personal vision for artistic endeavor.

Around 1923, Georgia wrote to her friend, the writer Sherwood Anderson, and described her intuitive but burning passion:

> I feel that a real living form is the natural result of the individual's effort to create the living thing out of the adventure of his spirit into the unknown, where it has experienced something—felt something—it has not understood. And from that experience, comes the desire to make the unknown known.
>
> By unknown, I mean the thing that means so much to the person that he wants to put it down—clarify something he feels but does not clearly understand. . . .

Sometimes it is all working in the dark, but a working that must be done. . . . You musn't even think you won't succeed.

I feel a sort of fury when you say that you won't succeed. I want to shake you to your senses—shake such an idea out of you for always. . . . Making your unknown known is the important thing—and keeping the unknown always beyond you—catching crystalizing your simpler clearer vision of life . . . that you must always keep working to grasp. . . .

You and I don't know if our vision is clear in relation to our time or not. No matter what failure or success we may have, we will not know. But we can keep our own integrity—according to our own sense of balance with the world. [39]

When it concerned painting, Georgia pursued personal vision rather than the applause of critics. To outsiders, she sometimes appeared unreasonable in her artistic pursuits, but for Georgia, who needed reasonable? She passionately followed her vision and changed the direction of American art.

*B*y reading the stories in this book, it's apparent that I'm passionate about biographies. The desire ignited several years ago and hasn't subsided. I especially enjoy reading about creative and successful women: They inspire me to keep cultivating my small measure of talent with the hope that someday I might make a difference.

In the meantime and between writing assignments, I've read about authors, dancers, actresses, comediennes, photographers, stateswomen, philosophers, political prisoners, royal family members, and others. After finishing a dozen or so books, I realized what these women shared in common: They followed an unshakable, sometimes unreasonable urge to accomplish their goals. And with this single-mindedness, they impacted the world.

Their lives also have taught me about change.

Whether we decide to change ourselves or the world, we need a dose of unreasonableness to deafen ourselves to the critics, to keep going. Whatever the endeavor, there are always people with explanations for why we should stop, or why we can't or shouldn't or won't accomplish the task. But as long as our goals are worthy and God-inspired, we needn't listen to them.

As a weekend author, I've thought of this often and especially recently. Some people think I'm reclusive, but I know that in writing books, I'm walking through God's open door. And with the completion of this manuscript, I'll have accomplished a major life goal, changed the direction of my writing, and hopefully touched people's lives.

Besides, critics seldom know all of the facts. I take time off between projects, I still socialize with friends, I pursue hobbies, and putter around town. I know my life isn't all work and no play, but it still hurts when critics dig for dysfunctions. That's when I need to find comfort in God and friends who understand.

Whatever we work to accomplish, whatever we try to change, most likely critics will snipe at us. But don't worry. When they begin, we can remember and be inspired by Jesus, the author and finisher of our faith. He ignored the critics and utterly changed the world.

PERSONAL CHECKPOINT

1. Are there critics who don't want you to change? If so, what do they say?

2. Have these critics affected your desire to change? Explain.

GOD'S VIEWPOINT

Encouragement to keep pressing on:

I want to encourage you to fight hard for the faith that was given the holy people of God once and for all time.

Dear friends, remember what the apostles of our Lord Jesus Christ said before. They said to you, "In the last times there will be people who

*laugh about God, following their own evil desires which are against God."
These are the people who divide you, people whose thoughts are only of this
world, who do not have the Spirit.*

*But dear friends, use your most holy faith to build yourselves up,
praying in the Holy Spirit. Keep yourselves in God's love as you wait for
the Lord Jesus Christ with his mercy to give you life forever.*

*Show mercy to some people who have doubts. Take others out of the
fire, and save them. Show mercy mixed with fear to others, hating even
their clothes which are dirty from sin.*

*God is strong and can help you not to fall. He can bring you before
his glory without any wrong in you and can give you great joy. He is the
only God, the One who saves us. To him be glory, greatness, power, and
authority through Jesus Christ our Lord for all time past, now, and forever.
Amen.*

—Jude 3c, 17-25

YOUR RESPONSE

1. How can you respond to non-Christians who criticize your
   journey toward change?

2. How can you respond to Christians who misunderstood your
   desire to change?

ATTACKS FROM BEHIND HURT THE WORST

Spiritual warfare against our goal can happen when we least expect it.

hen Sharon's parents divorced, her life turned upside down and wouldn't right itself again. She had been raised in a Christian home, so her father's affair created a horrible dissonance that she couldn't reconcile in her teenage mind.

To cope, she rebelled. First, with alcohol. Next, with sex. Then with drugs.

"For years, Sharon seemed bent on her own destruction," says her mother, Annabella. "I tried everything imaginable—curfews, counseling, discipline—but nothing worked. When she became an adult, I finally had to love her for who she was: a drug addict."

Annabella also prayed. She prayed that Sharon would reach the end of herself, search for God, and finally change.

It didn't happen.

Sharon's problems worsened. She married an actor who wouldn't support her, and they gave birth to a son whom Sharon loved dearly but who added to their financial woes. Again, to cope, Sharon picked up a needle. Her husband left and grandparents took the child.

Without her baby, Sharon faced reality. She checked into a detox center and braved severe withdrawals with newborn determination. Six months later, drug-free and internally renewed, she left the center to start over again.

Annabella felt encouraged. Her prayers had been answered. Sharon revived her hope.

Within a few months, Sharon retrieved her son, started working again, and vowed to stay clean. A few months later, though, she asked the doctor about her son's persistent and perplexing symptoms. After numerous tests, he diagnosed the young boy's illness as inoperable cancer.

"It's been a terrible blow," says Annabella. "Just when Sharon started to change, she got hit from behind. We're still reeling from it."

When we're progressing toward the long-awaited goal of personal change, it's attacks from behind that hurt the worst. Especially when our destination stands clearly in sight and we're anticipating the war's end. By this time, we've let down our guard and we're looking ahead to celebration. Finally, we will have changed.

Then unexpectedly, tragedy hits. Suddenly, we're fighting harder than before, with hope and help too far from us and our strength rapidly dwindling.

While researching for this day's reading, a retired military man explained that there's no prepared tactic for when an enemy attacks from behind. "You aren't supposed to get into those situations," he said. "All you can do is pull together, try to fight back, and call for help."

That's in the physical world. In the spiritual realm, anything can happen, even when we think it's not supposed to—especially when we feel we've battled long enough. So we're smart to stay prepared.

"Put on the full armor of God so that you can fight against the devil's evil tricks," advised Paul. Then he described our devious enemy.

"Our fight is not against people on earth but against the rulers and authorities and the powers of this world's darkness, against the spiritual powers of evil in the heavenly world. That is why you need to put on God's full armor. Then on the day of evil you will be able to stand strong. And when you have finished the whole fight, you will still be standing" (Ephesians 6:11-13). And we will have changed.

✣

PERSONAL CHECKPOINT

1. As you approach your goal, are you prepared for unexpected spiritual battle?

2. Are you putting on the full armor of God? (Read the passage on page 119 for a description of our spiritual battle gear.)

GOD'S VIEWPOINT

About suffering and spiritual warfare:

My friends, do not be surprised at the terrible trouble which now comes to test you. Do not think that something strange is happening to you. But be happy that you are sharing in Christ's sufferings so that you will be happy and full of joy when Christ comes again in glory. When people insult you because you follow Christ, you are blessed, because the glorious Spirit, the Spirit of God, is with you. Do not suffer for murder, theft, or any other crime, nor because you trouble other people. But if you suffer because you are a Christian, do not be ashamed. Praise God because you wear that name.

Be humble under God's powerful hand so he will lift you up when the right time comes. Give all your worries to him, because he cares about you.

Control yourselves and be careful! The devil, your enemy, goes around like a roaring lion looking for someone to eat. Refuse to give in to him, by standing strong in your faith. You know that your Christian family all over the world is having the same kinds of suffering.

And after you suffer for a short time, God, who gives all grace, will make everything right. He will make you strong and support you and keep you from falling. He called you to share in his glory in Christ, a glory that will continue forever. All power is his forever and ever.
—1 Peter 4:12-16; 5:6-11a

So stand strong, with the belt of truth tied around your waist and the protection of right living on your chest. On your feet wear the Good News of peace to help you stand strong. And also use the shield of faith with which you can stop all the burning arrows of the Evil One. Accept God's salvation as your helmet, and take the sword of the Spirit, which is the word of God. Pray in the Spirit at all times with all kinds of prayers, asking for everything you need. To do this you must always be ready and never give up.

—Ephesians 6:14-18b

YOUR RESPONSE

1. What parts of the spiritual armor do you still need to put on?

2. How can you stay alert to spiritual warfare and attacks from behind?

THE NEW, IMPROVED YOU

Holding on to the progress you've made

esus Christ has promised to be our present Teacher and Guide. His voice is not hard to hear. His instruction is not hard to understand. If we are beginning to calcify what always should remain alive and growing, He will tell us. We can trust His teaching. If we are wandering off toward some wrong idea or unprofitable practice, He will guide us back. If we are willing to listen to the Heavenly Monitor, we will receive the instruction we need.

Our world is hungry for genuinely changed people. Leo Tolstoy observed, "Everybody thinks of changing humanity and nobody thinks of changing himself." Let us be among those who believe that the inner transformation of our lives is a goal worthy of our best effort. [40]

Richard J. Foster,
Celebration of Discipline

*S*nowflakes nipped my fingers that Saturday as I pulled an assortment of envelopes from my roadside mailbox.

Ah, the Christmas cards are finally arriving, I thought. Then while dodging ice patches leading to my front door, I shuffled envelopes and read return addresses. One card felt bunchy, and I squeezed it a few times, anticipating a newsletter from an out-of-state friend.

In the dining room with my coat barely off, I tore open the fat envelope, gave the card a cursory look and dug into freshly typed pages. I smiled, wondering why Becky hadn't produced a form letter. Her schedule usually groaned with activity, even without the holiday season upon us.

A few paragraphs later, I understood why my friend had communicated personally. She wrote:

There is some sad news . . . Meredith is divorcing her husband and has totally renounced her faith in Christ. It was very hard for me to learn that, for I have been a friend to Meredith for years. She stopped answering my calls in April, and during July-August, I learned about her decision. What can I say?

Looking at the page again, I mentally questioned, *What's gone wrong, Lord?* But the query fell back to me, listless and useless. It seemed too late to ask.

Through my adult years, several of my friends had defected from Christianity, but Meredith's departure puzzled me the most. For several years, she had been working hard at changing difficult personality traits and continually asked God to help her. She implored Him for a sincere and life-changing faith.

One night, I sat in a car with Meredith and prayed about a personal problem she couldn't shake off. A few days later, she described how, at a counseling session the next day, she had reached a breakthrough point and began experiencing new freedom. She gave God the credit.

I had been encouraged by Meredith's change and growth as a Christian, and now, a few years later, she had left God altogether.

*M*eredith's story underscores the fact that, even though we accomplish great personal change, we can lose ground if we don't protect the progress we've made.

Not all stories of loss turn as tragic as Meredith's. A writer I know once lost fifty pounds and sold a magazine article about how she did it. But by the time the article appeared in the magazine, she had gained the weight back. She laughed as she told me, but I detected pain in her eyes.

Once we've changed, the work doesn't end. We need to guard against losing it.

But still, we don't need to fear. As we keep watch over the progress we've gained, God keeps guard with us. He has said, "I will never leave you; I will never forget you." So we can be sure when we say, "I will not be afraid, because the Lord is my helper. People can't do anything to me" (Hebrews 13:5b-6).

❋

PERSONAL CHECKPOINT

Part Six will help you responsibly live with the personal changes that you make.

1. How have you progressed toward your goal to change?

2. How can you prepare to guard against losing the ground you've gained?

3. What spiritual disciplines could help you keep watch?

Day

M Is for Maturity

*We can alter our circumstances,
but that won't change us.*

S he leaned across the cafe table and whispered, "You know, sometimes I feel like I haven't grown up."

I resisted the urge to suck in my breath. Not Lani. I admired her so much. With no prior experience, she had risen from copywriter to producer to vice president of an advertising agency in a few years. She was humble, without compulsions, reasonable about her work. Not at all like me.

Soaking in what she had said, I finally gulped and asked, "What do you mean?"

"Well, other people our age are married. They have houses, kids, in-laws. Adult stuff. I don't."

Neither did I.

"I understand," I whispered back, disappointed that not even Lani felt adultlike.

For a year or so I had voiced apprehensions about singleness versus marriage, childhood versus adulthood. So many of my single friends felt that, despite their age, they hadn't arrived at maturity and that someday, somehow, we would all be exposed as impostors among the real grown-ups.

But then my friend Kimberly got married. In the first year she gained a husband, in-laws, a house, a baby. So when we dined out one evening, I wasn't ready for déjà vu.

"You know," she said, "I have a husband and a daughter now, and I still don't feel grown up. When will it ever happen?"

I didn't know. But since then I've pondered our perceptions of adulthood and maturity.

*T*rue to the American way, we've defined maturity by people, places, things. Hardly ever ourselves. But it's no wonder. Developing mature character traits can be difficult; it's easier to possess someone or something than to change what's inside us. So acquisition, rather than character, becomes the measure of maturity.

Except it's not working. We're still glancing over our shoulders, wondering if our true identities, our real character flaws, will leak out. We're producing emotionally stagnant adults who relate like children, despite what they own. We're creating addictive, abusive behavior. And when we're confronted with it, we're running away.

We're ever changing our circumstances but seldom changing ourselves.

That described me for years. Switching from job to job and home to home, I thought altering my circumstances and accumulating professional accomplishments would make me a better person. Instead, the pressure of switching locales intensified what needed to change inside of me. After the fifth job, I complained to a friend, "I can switch locations, but I always take myself with me!"

I knew I needed to slow down and change—to recover from the terrible loneliness of running away.

Covering up our problems gets lonely, which is much different from simply being alone. Aloneness can help us mature. "This is the essence of coming of age—to learn how to stand alone," wrote Anne Morrow Lindbergh in *Gift from the Sea*. "She must find her true center alone. She must become whole." [41]

It's been said that to be adult is to be alone. But with Christ we can say, "to be mature is to feel whole when we're alone." Throughout the Bible, godliness is defined by who we are as individuals rather than by who we're with, or what we do, or what we own, or what we know.

Christ said the merciful, the pure in heart, the peacemakers are blessed (Matthew 5:3-10). Paul said the mature fruit of the Spirit is love, joy, peace, patience, kindness goodness, faithfulness, gentleness, and self-control (Galatians 5:22). These qualities require following the Spirit, understanding ourselves, making internal changes, forgetting what the world thinks.

That can be tough, but it's rewarding. When we find these traits growing inside us, we've discovered the meaning of maturity, the essence of adulthood, the fruits of our efforts to change. But most of all, we're reflecting God's character, and He's quite grown up.

PERSONAL CHECKPOINT

1. How do you define maturity?

2. Is your desire to change related to a need for this maturity?

GOD'S VIEWPOINT

On growing in Christ:

We must become like a mature person, growing until we become like Christ and have his perfection.

Then we will no longer be babies. We will not be tossed about like a ship that the waves carry one way and then another. We will not be influenced by every new teaching we hear from people who are trying to fool us. They make plans and try any kind of trick to fool people into following the wrong path. No! Speaking the truth with love, we will grow up in every way into Christ, who is the head.

—*Ephesians 4:13b-15*

But the day of the Lord will come like a thief. The skies will disappear with a loud noise. Everything in them will be destroyed by fire, and the earth and everything in it will be burned up. In that way everything will be destroyed. So what kind of people should you be? You should live holy lives and serve God, as you wait for and look forward to the coming of the day of God. When that day comes, the skies will be destroyed with fire, and everything in them will melt with heat. But God made a promise to us, and we are waiting for a new heaven and a new earth where goodness lives.

Dear friends, since you already know about this, be careful. Do not let those evil people lead you away by the wrong they do. Be careful so you will not fall from your strong faith. But grow in the grace and knowledge of our Lord and Savior Jesus Christ. Glory be to him now and forever! Amen.

—2 Peter 3:10-13, 17-18

YOUR RESPONSE

1. How can you gauge whether you're spiritually mature?

2. Could your knowledge of the Lord's coming change your definition of maturity? Explain.

THE COST OF COMMITMENT

God changes us so we can help others.

*S*tephanie was a new Christian, and although I didn't know her well, she seemed fun-loving and eager to learn. One night at a Bible study, she asked me if I would mentor her spiritually. Her enthusiasm invaded me, and without thinking, I said yes.

The evening of our first study time together, I hurriedly finished washing dishes before she arrived. With hands immersed in water, the parable of the sower popped into my head. And with each additional swipe of a dish, the story pieced together and then wouldn't leave.

"Okay, Lord," I sighed. "If you want me to share this parable with Stephanie, I will. But I don't understand why."

After settling on the couch and chatting a while, I told Stephanie we could begin by reading a parable from the book of Luke, chapter eight. Her face paled when I read, "Some seed fell on rock, and when it began to grow, it died because it had no water" (v. 6).

When I finished, Stephanie stammered, "I think I'm the seed on the rock." I assured her that she could become a seed falling on good ground that "made a hundred times more" (v. 8) and told her how to grow as a Christian.

The next week, Stephanie jilted our scheduled time together. She didn't respond to my phone messages, and I never heard from her again. I suspect when Stephanie discovered that Christianity required commitment, she decided it wasn't worth it.

*W*hen I think of Stephanie's change of mind, I can't help but think of myself. Sure, I'm still a Christian, while who knows what happened to her. But as I work through issues of change, I realize how easily I can warm up to God when I need Him—and how swiftly I can draw back after He's granted my requests.

I too soon forget that a relationship with God takes a two-way commitment.

God saves us from sin and changes us because He loves us, but not so we can squander it on ourselves. Once we've received His grace, He asks us to multiply it a hundredfold in the lives of others.

We change so that, in turn, we can help others. Bible teacher Hannah Whithall Smith explained this spiritual exchange:

> Many people seem to think that the only thing proposed in religion is to improve the "old man," that is, the flesh; and that the way to do this is to discipline and punish it until it is compelled to behave. Hence comes the asceticism of the Buddhist and others; and hence, also, comes the idea that the "cross" for Christians consists in the painful struggles of this helpless "old man" to do the will of God, a will which in the very nature of things the flesh cannot understand or love.
>
> But a true comprehension of the religion of Christ shows us that what is really meant is the death of this old man and the birth in us of a "new creature," begotten of God, whose tastes and instincts are all in harmony with God, *and to whom the doing of God's will must be, and cannot help being, a joy and a delight.*
>
> It is not the old man thwarted and made miserable by being compelled to submit to a will it dislikes, but it

is a new man, "created in Christ Jesus unto good works," and therefore doing these good works with ease and pleasure; a new nature, of divine origin, which is in harmony with the divine will, and therefore delights to do it. [42]

With this understanding, we can say with the psalmist, "I delight to do Thy will, O my God" (Psalm 40:8a; NASB).

PERSONAL CHECKPOINT

1. What are your goals for desiring to change?

2. Through the change process, have you asked God about His will for you?

GOD'S VIEWPOINT

Praise for God's help:

> *I waited patiently for the LORD.*
> *He turned to me and heard my cry.*
> *He lifted me out of the pit of destruction,*
> *out of the sticky mud.*
> *He stood me on a rock*
> *and made my feet steady.*
> *He put a new song in my mouth,*
> *a song of praise to our God.*
> *Many people will see this and worship him.*
> *Then they will trust the LORD.*
>
> *Happy is the person*
> *who trusts the LORD,*
> *who doesn't turn to those who are proud*
> *or to those who worship false gods.*
> *LORD my God, you have done many miracles.*
> *Your plans for us are many.*

If I tried to tell them all,
there would be too many to count.

You do not want sacrifices and offerings.
But you have made a hole in my ear
to show that my body and life are yours.
You do not ask for burnt offerings
and sacrifices to take away sins.
Then I said, "Look, I have come.
It is written about me in the book.
My God, I want to do what you want.
Your teachings are in my heart."
                              —Psalm 40:1-8

YOUR RESPONSE

1. How can you use your changed life to help others?

2. When and how could you begin?

BELIEVING IN
A BETTER YOU

***When people won't believe we've changed,
we can trust the God who changed us.***

*Y*ou married folks can come through this line," the usher
said as he pointed me toward the wedding cake and
punch. I looked back at Terry, stifled a laugh and followed the
reception line. I had given up on explanations.

Terry is a single friend I used to call my "escort service"
when I still lived in my hometown. Seeing us together, people
often misnamed him as my husband, my boyfriend, or "relationship." But Terry never flinched. We knew what few people
believed: We were just friends.

("I'm proud to be seen with you," he once said. And the
misnomers bothered me less.)

We weren't always so secure in our friendship. When I met
Terry, I developed a colossal crush on him—as have many women
since. I attended his Bible study with less thought for the lesson
than for the teacher—and it bothered me because I felt emotionally fragile and couldn't face a possible rejection.

After a couple of months of agony, I blurted my feelings to
an older Christian woman who took me seriously.

"Judy," she said, "let's start praying about him, asking God to reveal what the relationship should be."

I agreed, never suspecting His answer. In less than two weeks, my clinging, can't-think-of-anyone-but-him emotions left. They had been replaced with the confidence that Terry could be my friend.

Remarkably, I had changed.

As with anything in God's economy, what appeared to be negative turned positive. His answer gave us freedom, direction, protection. I knew my boundaries with Terry; I had been shielded from the wounds of loving the wrong person.

After that, I thought the struggle was over. But then well-intentioned friends and strangers wouldn't believe me. They would smile and nod, convinced that I denied deeper feelings, that I couldn't enjoy a man's company without winding up at the altar or at least in his bed.

For some reason, they couldn't or wouldn't believe in real change.

*Y*ou're still the same old Judy I've always known."

Those are the last words I want to hear. Even when it's meant as a compliment from a longtime friend, that assessment sinks me. I want people to know that I'm different, that I've struggled to get better, that I've changed.

Instead, they casually negate my efforts.

I have to remind myself that people's assumptions can emerge from a lack of information, not from the fact that I haven't changed. For example, several months ago, a friend said to me, "Oh, Judy, you're just always working!"

My sensitive antenna picked up on that one. For the last two years I had consciously chosen to work less. I had quit doing overtime at the office, taken few writing assignments, and accomplished a lot of nothing. But Donna didn't know that. She lived in another town. She hadn't seen me for a few years. She believed old information.

God, help me, I thought. *I don't want to feel slighted by her assessment.* Then without thinking, I told Donna that she was wrong, that she needed to update her facts, that I had worked hard at change and I wanted her to believe it.

No problem, she said. She would believe in the new me.

Sometimes changing people's attitudes about our changing selves can be as simple as telling them the truth. Or letting them observe us for a while. Other times, people just refuse to believe it. They rub our noses in the past, eager to point out what resembles that "same old woman."

If we've honestly changed, then it's time to believe it's their problem and not ours—that maybe they haven't forgiven us, even if we've asked them to; that our new self points to their old, unaltered problems; or that change, in general, threatens them.

We can embrace these assertions not with revenge, but with a surrendered soul that lets God work in their hearts. We can ask Him to change their attitudes, just as He's changed ours, and we can remember that transforming them is the Holy Spirit's job, not ours. And when we leave their attitudes to God, we're free to enjoy the new person we've become.

PERSONAL CHECKPOINT

1. Is someone refusing to believe that you're changing or have changed? If so, why might this person refuse to believe it?

2. How have you felt about this person? Why?

GOD'S VIEWPOINT

How life changes when we know Christ:

The love of Christ controls us, because we know that One died for all, so all have died. Christ died for all so that those who live would not continue to live for themselves. He died for them and was raised from the dead so that they would live for him.

From this time on we do not think of anyone as the world does. In the past we thought of Christ as the world thinks, but we no longer think of him in that way. If anyone belongs to Christ, there is a new creation.

The old things have gone; everything is made new! All this is from God. Through Christ, God made peace between us and himself, and God gave us the work of telling everyone about the peace we can have with him. God was in Christ, making peace between the world and himself. In Christ, God did not hold the world guilty of its sins. And he gave us this message of peace. So we have been sent to speak for Christ. It is as if God is calling to you through us. We speak for Christ when we beg you to be at peace with God. Christ had no sin, but God made him become sin so that in Christ we could become right with God.

—2 Corinthians 5:14-21

YOUR RESPONSE

1. Have you thanked God for the old things that have passed away? If not, how about now?

2. How can you respond to people who don't believe that you're changing or have changed?

Day

NOBODY LOVES A CRITIC

**When we finally change, it doesn't
mean we can criticize those who haven't.**

or reasons I've forgotten, I stayed away from the office
that morning. And after a late breakfast, I switched on
the television for background noise while tackling housework. A
familiar voice boomed from the tube.

Donahue, I surmised and entered the bathroom, cleanser
and scrub brush in hand. *I wonder what he's got people riled up about
today.*

I turned a faucet handle and over splashing and scouring,
the T.V. blurted an answer.

That day's entertainment began with a lineup of guests
espousing the joys of weight loss. Then to spice their lean-cuisine
stories—and audience reactions—Donahue pitted them against a
double-chinned lady who insisted that fat is beautiful.

I left a half-clean sink to view the woman. With four ex-fat-
ties against her, I knew she would wind up emotionally carved to
the bone. And for the next half hour, I dipped in and out of the
bathroom, watching the screen more than the porcelain.

My sympathies sided with the fat lady. At one point, her husband, thin as a popsicle stick, emerged from the audience to

deliver his homily, Why I Love Her Just the Way She Is. I admired his devotion.

But the overweight wife couldn't bask in his love for long. Immediately another female guest countered with a hard-edged sermon about What's Terribly Wrong with Obese People. I resisted her arrogance.

Just when I had nominated the slimmed-down lady as Most Prejudiced Person of the Year, she concluded: "I was right to lose the weight, and I give all of the credit to the Lord!"

With scattered whoops from the audience, the formerly obese lady's reputation dwindled to nothing. And in my opinion, so did the Lord's.

Actually, there's no faux pas great enough to damage the Lord's reputation or stifle His plans. Yet, because of our opinions, we can hurtle potshots that damage people's attitudes toward God and us.

Often it's when we've finally "gotten the victory" and we want strugglers around us to get it, too. But for various mixed-up reasons, we accomplish the opposite of our intentions, and after we've conquered a sin, we condemn it in others. So the ex-smoker criticizes her puffing colleague, the reformed gossip lectures a storytelling neighbor, the ex-sedentary can't stomach an out-of-shape friend, and the Christian who's finally mastered a devotional life looks down on her undisciplined spiritual sister.

The basic story isn't new. Twenty-five centuries ago, Aesop told a brief fable about a wolf and some shepherds. The animal peered into a hut to watch the shepherds chomp on a mutton joint.

"These shepherds seem mightily pleased with themselves today. But later, when they are full and no longer need the mutton, they will condemn me for doing the same thing," sneered the wolf. [43]

While the fable's plot misses compelling action, the author's moral hits our hearts: We are too apt to condemn in others what we have done ourselves. And nobody loves a critic.

An even wiser Man explained: "For out of the fullness . . . of the heart the mouth speaks" (Matthew 12:34b; AMPLIFIED). So when we ask, "I've got it together; why don't you?" our tongues really wag about our cold hearts.

On the other hand, Paul told the Ephesians: "When you talk, do not say harmful things, but say what people need—words that will help others become stronger. . . . Be kind and loving to each other, and forgive each other just as God forgave you in Christ" (Ephesians 4:29, 32).

True kindness, love, and forgiveness spring from compassion, from an act that says, "I may be victorious, but I will not condemn you; I remember what it's like to struggle." The key to compassion rests in a true spirit of humility, usually produced from suffering through the change process ourselves.

Missionary Amy Carmichael knew suffering and wrote: "What can we do to help? If only Calvary be the background of our living, if only we continue with our Lord in Gethsemane, if only every common word and deed, our whole bearing, our whole being is steeped in the spirit that was His when He set His face steadfastly to go to Jerusalem, then those who look to us will see that Cross and be drawn into that fellowship.

"There is no other way to help them. There is no other way to be helped ourselves."[44]

❀

Personal Checkpoint

1. Are you critical or compassionate toward people who need to change?

2. How do you treat people who struggle with the same sin that you've fought against?

God's Viewpoint

How we're to help each other:

Brothers and sisters, if someone in your group does something wrong, you who are spiritual should go to that person and gently help make him right again. But be careful, because you might be tempted to sin, too. By helping each other with your troubles, you truly obey the law of Christ. If anyone thinks he is important when he really is not, he is only fooling himself.

Each person should judge his own actions and not compare himself with others. Then he can be proud for what he himself has done. Each person must be responsible for himself.

Anyone who is learning the teaching of God should share all the good things he has with his teacher.

Do not be fooled: You cannot cheat God. People harvest only what they plant. If they plant to satisfy their sinful selves, their sinful selves will bring them ruin. But if they plant to please the Spirit, they will receive eternal life from the Spirit. We must not become tired of doing good. We will receive our harvest of eternal life at the right time if we do not give up. When we have the opportunity to help anyone, we should do it. But we should give special attention to those who are in the family of believers.

—Galatians 6:1-10

YOUR RESPONSE

1. How can you express love and kindness to those still mired in sin?

2. What could result from a lack of compassion toward these people?

GOING FOR BROKE

With God, we can risk a lifetime of openness to change.

 e've reached the end of this book, but I hope it's just the beginning of our commitment to change. As we live in these sin-filled bodies, God wants to keep molding us into His image. Spiritual growth lasts for a lifetime—and it requires a go-for-broke openness to change.

Several years ago, I worked in the same company as Joseph Bayly, a writer whose work and life I admired. Joe stayed open to change, and when he died, a crowded funeral service attested to the many people he had touched with this attitude.

Earlier in life, Joe wrote "A Psalm requesting faith," which characterized his life until the end. It is my prayer for all of us as we continue our journey toward change:

> Give me courage Lord
> to take risks
> not the usual ones
> respected
> necessary

relatively safe
but those I could avoid
the go for broke ones.
I need courage
not just because
I may fall on my face
or worse
but others seeing me
a sorry spectacle
if it should happen
will say
he didn't know what he was doing
or he's foolhardy
or he's old enough to know
you lead from the side
instead of letting yourself be caught
in wild stampede.
Give me courage Lord
to take unnecessary risks
live at tension
instead of opting out.
Give me the guts to put up
instead of shutting up.
When it comes right down to it
Lord
I choose to be Your failure
before anyone else's success.
Keep me from reneging
on my choice. [44]

PERSONAL CHECKPOINT

1. What has encouraged and frustrated you about working toward change?

2. How do you feel about a lifetime of personal change?

GOD'S VIEWPOINT

How to walk with God for a lifetime:

Happy are those who don't listen to the wicked,
*   who don't go where sinners go,*
*   who don't do what evil people do.*
They love the LORD's teachings,
*   and they think about those teachings day and*
*   night.*
They are strong, like a tree planted by a river.
*   The tree produces fruit in season,*
*   and its leaves don't die.*
Everything they do will succeed.

But wicked people are not like that.
*   They are like chaff that the wind blows away.*
So the wicked will not escape God's punishment.
*   Sinners will not worship with God's people.*
This is because the LORD takes care of his people,
*   but the wicked will be destroyed.*
                                    —Psalm 1

YOUR RESPONSE

1. How can you stay open to a lifetime of change?

2. What personal changes do you want to make during your lifetime?

Notes

Part 1: STARTLING INTO THE TRUTH

1. Anne Wilson Schaef, *When Society Becomes an Addict* (San Francisco: Harper & Row, 1987), p. 67.
2. Schaef, p. 67.
3. Melody Beattie, *Denial* (Center City, MN: Hazeldon, 1986), p. 4.
4. Sophocles, *Antigone*, lines 276-77. *The Dramas of Sophocles*, trans. Sir George Young, (1888), p. 16.
5. Herman Melville, *Billy Budd, Sailor and Other Stories* (New York: Bantam Books, 1962), pp. 95-130.
6. David Seamands, *Healing for Damaged Emotions* (Wheaton: Victor Books, 1983), p. 21.
7. Evelyn Christenson, *Lord, Change Me!* (Wheaton: Victor Books, 1983), p. 90.
8. David Swartz, *Dancing with Broken Bones* (Colorado Springs: NavPress, 1987), p. 82.
9. Colleen Townsend Evans, *A Deeper Joy* (Old Tappan, NJ: Fleming H. Revell Company, 1982), p. 42.
10. J.R. Miller, D.D., *In Green Pastures* (Camden, NJ: Thomas Nelson, 1969), p. 72.

Part 2: A TRUE VIEW OF YOU

11. Penelope J. Stokes, *So What If You've Failed?* (Colorado Springs: NavPress, 1990), p. 23.
12. Isabel Russell, *Katharine and E.B. White: An Affectionate Memoir* (New York: W.W. Norton & Company, 1988), pp. 52-53.
13. Margaret Bourke-White, *Portrait of Myself* (New York: Simon and Schuster, 1963), p. 21.

14. Bourke-White, p. 11.
15. Catherine Marshall, *The Prayers of Peter Marshall* (Lincoln, VA: Chosen Books, 1954), pp. 19-20.
16. Mary S. Lovell, *Straight on Till Morning: The Biography of Beryl Markham* (New York: St. Martin's Press, 1987), n.p.
17. This reading first appeared in *Getting a Grip on Guilt* by Judith Couchman (Colorado Springs: NavPress, 1990), pp. 11-13; 17. Used by permission.

Part 3: WHEN THE INSIDES SPILL OUT

18. Paul Tournier, *The Meaning of Persons* (San Francisco: Harper & Row), 1957, pp. 54-55.
19. H.R. Rookmaaker, *The Creative Gift* (Westchester, IL: Cornerstone Books, 1981), p. 134.
20. Henry David Thoreau, *Walden and "Civil Disobedience"* (New York: Signet Classics, 1960), p. 10.
21. Harriet Goldhor Lerner, Ph.D., *The Dance of Anger* (New York: Harper & Row, 1985), pp. 2-3.
22. Stephanie E., *Shame Faced* (Center City, MN: Hazeldon, 1986), p. 1.
23. A. A. Milne, *Winnie-the-Pooh* (New York: E.P. Dutton & Co., 1954), pp. 72-74.
24. Edith Hamilton, *Mythology* (New York: The New American Library, 1969), pp. 70-72.
25. Dr. Larry Crabb, *Inside Out* (Colorado Springs: NavPress, 1988), p. 201.

Part 4: STUMBLING TOWARD FREEDOM

26. Lerner, p. 12.
27. Lewis Carroll, *Alice's Adventures in Wonderland and Through the Looking-Glass* (New York: The New American Library, 1960), pp. 90-91.
28. John Newton, "Amazing Grace," from *Hymns of the Christian Life* (Harrisburg, PA: Christian Publications, Inc., 1936), p. 101.
29. Andrew Morton, *Diana: Her True Story* (New York: Simon & Shuster, 1992), pp. 73-74.
30. Eleanor Perényi, *Green Thoughts: A Writer in the Garden* (New York: Random House, 1981), p. 80.

31. A.W. Tozer, *Man: The Dwelling Place of God* (Harrisburg, PA: Christian Publications, Inc., 1966), pp. 51-52.
32. "Warming Up" by Karen Burton Mains, *Sunday Digest,* January 13, 1985 (Elgin, IL: David C. Cook), p. 3.

Part 5: SMARTER, NOT HARDER

33. Mark I. Bubeck, *The Adversary* (Chicago: Moody Press, 1975), pp. 37, 73.
34. Robert B. Grossman, "The Weekend Athlete: Avoiding Injuries," *Total Health,* August 1989, p. 20.
35. John Sherrill, *My Friend, the Bible* (Lincoln, VA: Chosen Books, 1978), pp. 55-56.
36. "'Mastery' and 'Helpless' Styles in Adolescents," *The Brown University Child Behavior and Development Letter,* November 1990, p. 3.
37. Christina Robb, "Models of Myth," *Gazette Telegraph,* 25 June 1992, sec. E, p. 1.
38. John Bartlett, *Bartlett's Familiar Quotations* (Boston: Little, Brown and Company, 1980), p. 823.
39. Jack Cowart and Juan Hamilton, *Georgia O'Keeffe: Arts and Letters* (Washington, D.C.: National Gallery of Art, 1987), pp. 174-175.

Part 6: THE NEW, IMPROVED YOU

40. Richard J. Foster, *Celebration of Discipline* (San Francisco: Harper & Row, 1978), p. 9.
41. Anne Morrow Lindbergh, *Gift from the Sea* (New York: Random House, 1975), p. 96.
42. Hannah Whitall Smith, *The Common Sense Teaching of the Bible* (Old Tappan, NJ: Fleming H. Revell, 1985), pp. 112-113.
43. *Aesop's Fables* (New York: Grosset and Dunlap, 1947), p. 230.
44. Amy Carmichael, *Whispers of His Power* (Old Tappan, NJ: Fleming H. Revell, 1982), p. 57.
45. Joseph Bayly, *Psalms of My Life* (Wheaton, IL: Tyndale House Publishers, 1973), pp. 47-48. Used by permission.

About the Author

Judith Couchman is Director of Product Development for the Periodicals Group of NavPress and a free-lance writer. Through her writing, she wants to "encourage people to find help and comfort in a loving and forgiving God."

Judith has published many times in magazines and curriculum publications and formerly worked as the editor of *Sunday Digest* and also *Christian Life*. She's taught writing at conferences around the United States and has received top honors from professional organizations for her work in secondary education, religious publishing, and corporate communications.

With this release, Judith has published five books. She holds a B.S. in education and an M.A. in journalism and putters in her flower gardens while procrastinating on deadlines. She lives in Colorado Springs, Colorado.